The best lead for your sales pipeli[...] ferral-generating principles are taugh[...] must-read for anyone who wants to stay ahead of their competition and stay top of mind with their prospects and customers.

Jeb Blount, CEO of Sales Gravy, Inc., and Author of *Fanatical Prospecting* and *People Buy You*

Kody's new book *The Power of Human Connection* will transform the way people do business. There is nothing like it. It is real life success stories of a vastly underused philosophy and skill. The success stories alone make this book worth reading. The results business owners are getting will astound you! This will become one of the most highly recommended books for transforming business as we know it.

Jordan Adler, Author, Entrepreneur, Master Networker

The Power of Human Connection is one of Kody B's best creations yet. The examples set within these pages teach how success comes from strengthening personal and business relationships. You'll learn a relationship strategy that, if put into practice, will organically explode your word-of-mouth referrals—the most powerful of all advertising. Kody's knowledge and words will inspire you on everything you need to increase the heart of your relationships and business.

Dave & Lori Smith, Multiple Business Owners and Relationship Marketing Experts, Co-owners, Eagles Flight LLC

The book of secrets on how to build an extraordinary life is revealed in Kody's latest treasure. Since following his work over the last 10-plus years, I am grateful for his teachings. *The Power of Human Connection* will further everyone's need to grow taller and stronger. I suggest you grab a copy and an extra 100 to share with the world.

Jay McHugh, LAER Realty Partners

The Power of Human Connection will lead you on a journey to greatness, both personally and professionally. It's a book for everyone in business. It teaches the true avenue to success: build relationships, love people, celebrate life, and be of service to others.

Gayle Zientek, Broker/Owner/Realtor,
Network Team Homes Realty

Masterful. Kody Bateman delivers the secrets of relationship marketing with a knockout punch. His latest book will be the cornerstone of every entrepreneur's library. We learn from real life examples as Kody pulls back the curtain on relationship marketing secrets and practices that simply transform businesses. A fantastic read and authentic look at the way businesses and people can prosper together.

Peter Anthony Wynn, Founder of YouWillChangetheWorld.com

Kody has inspired us since 2005. He has a tremendous way of writing, encouraging you to first identify yourself and know that you always attract what you give out. We are in the real estate and the automotive consulting business, and creating strong relationships has always been our focus. SendOutCards' system brings traditional values into today's high-tech world.

Bob & Betty Ann Golden, Golden Greetings, Inc.,
Trainers, Speakers, and Inspirational Relationship Mentors

The Power of Human Connection takes an everyday subject and turns it into a compelling read that sizzles with brave energy. It's a must-read to understand the importance of building relationships not only in your personal life, but also for the success of your business. Kody Bateman does an incredible job of teaching how the power of human connection affects our lives every day. He emphasizes the fact that life is nothing more than building relationships and sharing ideas. Once relationships are formed, the sky is the limit.

Steve Schulz, author of *Yes, Sometimes it is About the Money*

THE POWER OF
HUMAN
CONNECTION

How *Relationship Marketing* is Transforming the Way People Succeed

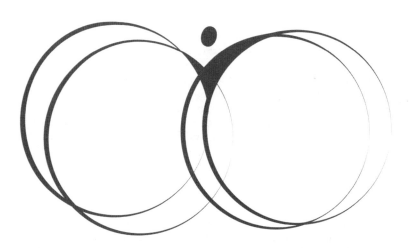

KODY BATEMAN

FOREWORD BY IVAN MISNER, PH.D.
NEW YORK TIMES BESTSELLING AUTHOR & FOUNDER OF BNI

Copyright © 2018 Kody Bateman

All rights reserved. No part of this publication may be reproduced, distributed or transmitted in any form or by any means, including photocopying, recording, or other electronic or mechanical methods, without the prior written permission of the publisher, except in the case of brief quotations embodied in critical reviews and certain other noncommercial uses permitted by copyright law. For permission requests, write to info@kodybateman.com, Attention: Permissions Coordinator.

Editing, design: Melody Marler, Publishing Concierge
Cover design, interior graphics: Ryan Tranmer
Printed in the United States of America

The Power of Human Connection: How Relationship Marketing is Transforming the Way People Succeed / Kody Bateman,—1st ed.
ISBN 978-1-936677-42-9 (paperback)
ISBN 978-1-936677-43-6 (eBook)

EAGLE ONE
PUBLISHING

CONTENTS

SECTION 3
Why the Relationship You Build
with Yourself is Most Important

Big Picture Conclusion

How Relationship Marketing is Transforming
the Way People Succeed

A Tribute to Relationships

When I was eight years old, I joined a youth basketball league and was assigned to a team where I played point guard. I was the guy who dribbled the ball up the court. The other guard on that team was Dave Smith. We played several games together and became friends. Dave lived only a block away from me, so it was easy for us to meet and hang out together.

We rode our bikes all around the neighborhoods, sometimes many miles away from home. We played sports, rode motorcycles, swam in pools and canals, and were always active outside, finding adventure as kids did back then.

That was well over 40 years ago and Dave and I are still the best of friends. I was with Dave in a high school cafeteria on the day he met the love of his life. I remember watching him mouth three words to her from across the table: "I love you." That was his first interaction with Lori. They have been together ever since, and they now have three children and nine grandchildren.

Dave and Lori got married young, had their kids when they were young, and started their own business when they were young. Dave learned the masonry trade while working for his father. He was given leadership responsibility at a very young age and mastered his craft. He and Lori ran a very successful masonry business for many years. They decided about 12 years before this writing to leave the construction business for good. They joined Jodi and I on our crusade to help people create and nurture relationships in business and in life.

You can tell a lot about the depth of relationship by the loyalty people may or may not portray. There are many who will enter your life and then leave it based on what they can get from your relationship. There are others who will remain, because giving to the relationship is the consistent focus from both parties.

Through the victories and the defeats, Dave and Lori have always been there. They have remained focused on how they can serve our cause of creating human connection. Through that service, they have mastered their craft as relationship marketing experts. Dave currently heads up our Sendogo business where CRMs can integrate with our relationship marketing system.

We have not always agreed on things, and we have even weathered heated debates and misunderstandings. But in the end, we always accept our differences, embrace our common goals and interests, and nurture a friendship that has seen us through 40-plus years of life adventure. That is what a true relationship looks like.

There is a picture of Dave and I on our dirt bikes found on page 111 in this book. From Jodi and I to Dave and Lori, we pay tribute to friendship and to an example of the power of genuine human connection.

Kody Bateman

Foreword

I spoke at a business conference in London recently. There were 900 people in the audience from about 500 different professions. I asked, "How many of you are here today hoping to maybe, just possibly, sell something?" All 900 people raised their hands.

"OK, second question," I continued. "How many of you are here today hoping to maybe, just possibly, buy something?"

Not one hand went up.

This is what I call the networking disconnect. People show up at networking meetings wanting to sell, but they're not open to buying.

In 1985, I founded BNI (Business Network International). BNI has grown to become the largest networking organization in the world, with about 9.5 million referrals generated every year driving about $13.8 billion worth of business and referrals for our members.

With BNI, our core operating philosophy is that business is largely done by relationships. We can stay connected with people in so many ways—email, texting, social media and other online communication methodologies. But all of the tech-driven communication has now become almost mundane. It's the type of touch people are used to. So now, actually getting something in the mail is unusual and it makes you stand out in your recipients' eyes. I'm not sure I would have said that 30 years ago! At that time, all communication was done either with a phone call or through the mail.

Early in the 80s I read the book *Megatrends* by John Naisbitt. One of his main messages was that as society moves toward high-tech, society must evolve to also become high-touch. As we become more inward and isolated by technology, it's increasingly important to connect with people. With his marketing business, Kody Bateman has merged high-tech and high-touch eloquently, and integrates it effectively with building relationships. Companies like his are the fruition of that early vision of high-tech, high-touch.

So we've come full circle. Kody has employed technology to make something very personal. Getting tangible items in the mail is very powerful, and it's a great example of the power of connection. Adding the photograph and handwriting font makes the product ultra-personal. I meet thousands of people over the course of a year, so while I may not recall someone's name, if I get a card with their photo on it, I am easily able to recall the person or conversation.

One of the dilemmas we hear over and over again from BNI members is, "How do you follow up with people?" First of all, the follow-up you will actually DO is the best! You've got to follow up. And I think one of the most effective is the handwritten note. The problem for me—and I suspect for others—is that I stink at handwritten notes. My handwriting's not that good, and it's shocking how reliant I've become on spellcheck. What I love about Kody's relationship marketing product is that you can make a follow-up card in your own handwriting, from your computer. You haven't actually had to hand-write it, but it looks like you did. To me that's just brilliant—the epitome of high-tech, high-touch.

Networking isn't supposed to work like a get-rich-quick scheme. It's a way to build a solid foundation for a long-term business. The focus is on building relationships and passing each other referrals; that allows reciprocation to take care of itself.

It's a shame this philosophy isn't taught in colleges and universities; we don't teach networking or relationship marketing. So what naturally happens when people begin to build businesses is that they usually go straight into sales mode and use networking as a face-to-face cold-calling opportunity instead of a relationship-building opportunity, which is what it should be when it's done right.

When I started BNI 33 years ago, it wasn't my goal to change the world. It was my goal to change an individual life, to help one person, and then another person, and then another person; you change the world by changing individual lives. We all have people who are in our stories and maybe what they do is a simple little thing, but it changes your life immensely. I don't often ask, "Who's in your story?" But I do like to ask, "Whose story are you in?" To me, that's the real question.

Who's out there saying, "Boy, this person made a huge difference in my life?" That's when you know you're changing the world and you're doing it just a little bit at a time. That's all I've ever tried to do is change it just a little bit at a time, and I truly feel that's what Kody's relationship marketing company is doing for the world, one card at a time. His system is also retraining people to reach out in kindness and with the pure intent of connection, to give and not to get.

I've known Kody for many years. BNI has had a strategic relationship with SendOutCards for most of that time. Kody is an outstanding leader. He continually does big things that turn conventional marketing wisdom on its head.

Remember, networking is more about farming than it is about hunting. It's about cultivating relationships. The relationship-building process is often a slow one, but I promise you, it will be one of the most rewarding and lucrative ways you will ever find to build your businesses.

Ivan Misner, Ph.D.
New York Times Bestselling
Author and Founder of BNI

Why Human Connection is Everything

Chances are you purchased this book because you want to learn what relationship marketing is and how it can help you succeed in your business.

I learned a long time ago that for me to teach you what relationship marketing truly is, I must first *leverage what you want from me.* And that is information and systems that help you generate referrals, new business and incremental sales. After all, that's what marketing is all about, right? You are part of a vast marketplace that wants and needs to find success in generating business.

So that is exactly what I'm going to do. I will leverage your wants by giving you that information. I will introduce you to systems, and I will share countless stories and steps on how to implement a successful relationship marketing plan. I will teach you the power of the tangible touch and why that is essential to your marketing plan in today's world. I will show you how, with minimal but consistent investment, you can generate referral sales that most people only dream of. I won't be sharing theories.

I will be sharing facts backed by countless examples of people who have generated the results you seek. But to do all that, I need to *inspire you on what you need from me.* And that includes a philosophy and a system for human connection.

You will notice this book has a bunch of words on the front cover. The subhead, *How Relationship Marketing is Transforming the Way People Succeed,* is what you want from me. The title, *The Power of Human Connection,* is what you need from me.

Human connection is the driving force behind making a relationship marketing plan that works. You will read numerous times in this book that relationship marketing is about the first word, not the second. Marketing is what you want from me. Relationship is what you need from me.

Human connection is all about the relationship, not just relationship with others but also relationship with self. The most powerful form of human connection takes place around the universal law of attraction; what you send out to self and others is what will come back to you.

You will see this as a common theme from cover to cover. Make no mistake, this is a business and marketing book that will generate massive success if you follow its teachings. But it's also a relationship and personal development book that will transform your life.

When I took on this project, I wanted to make sure people saw it as a business book. I wanted a title that caught people's attention but also resonated as a professional business message. *That's what the marketplace wants.* It also needed to convey the theme and philosophy of human connectivity. It needed to resonate with the "what you send out comes back to you" message. ***That's what the marketplace needs.***

My team and I had a lot of interesting conversation about creating the right title. We even discussed some title concepts with an audience of 210 people attending one of my relationship marketing summits in Scottsdale, Arizona. First, I told them I was writing a new book about relationship marketing and was trying to come up with a creative title. To set up the questions I told them I wanted to do something with the word "karma."

I explained that karma is nothing more than cause and effect: what you send out comes back to you. To master relationship marketing you simply need to send out positivity and appreciation to others. Karma is a creative and accurate word that resonates with not only what you should do, but also with what you shouldn't do.

If you focus only on what you can *get* from a relationship, that creates bad karma; if you focus on what you can *give* to a relationship, you create good karma. This is the essence of what true relationship marketing is all about. So karma is a great word to describe the activities necessary to succeed.

I also explained that the word karma sparked negative emotions for many people. Why? Simply because most people send out negativity, so karma becomes a bad word for them.

To illustrate this, I asked them to finish this sentence out loud: "Karma is a _____." Sure enough, many of those in the audience quickly said, "Bitch."

This is a widely known phrase all over the world, and I have been puzzled by it for years. Why do people feel this way? If people think karma is a bitch, then they associate karma with something bad that might happen to them. Based on the definition, that means most people are sending out negative things, and just as they expect, karma simply returns negative results.

Unfortunately, in a negative society, this proves to be true more times than not. In fact, studies have shown 87 percent of everything you hear is negative. That's a whole lot of negative programming. Chances are you may be sending out negativity in the way of your thoughts, feelings, words and deeds. This may be why people experience negative emotions when they hear the word karma.

I continued with my presentation to the audience, saying, "Based on what we are discussing here today, we all know the statement 'karma is a bitch' is not true. So what do you think of the title, *Karma is Not a Bitch*?" Everyone cheered. Then I told the crowd my friend Dave Smith, who was in the back running the production, had come up with a slight twist to that name. "I'm going to say it and, based on how loud you cheer, we will know if you like it better than the first one. Is everyone ready?" I paused, and then said, "*Make Karma Your Bitch.*" The crowd went crazy with that version, so we knew they liked it better than the first one.

I know some of you love that title and some of you take offense to it. We didn't want half of the marketplace taking offense, so we figured we were close, but not quite there yet. I told the crowd we were going to continue forward with the course we were teaching. If any of you come up with other ideas, I said, then share them and we will see how the crowd likes it.

We went forward with the day. I talked about our usual principles on relationship marketing and personal development—

things like the importance of tangible appreciation touches including thank you, birthday and holiday cards, keep in touch cards and gifts; focusing on relationship first, at least 80 percent of the time and marketing second, about 20 percent of the time; not asking for the referral but deserving it; and creating genuine connections and truly caring about people you do business with. We showed case studies, role-played on the stage, and showed examples of how businesses from numerous niches creatively communicate and appreciate their client base. And of course we shared stories about the massive results these businesses experience by using our system.

So as this interactive discussion was going on, my good friend Mark Whaley, who was in the audience, raised his hand and said, "I have the name for your book. *Make Karma your Niche.*" The crowd went into thunderous applause. It was a mic drop moment. It appeared we had landed on the title.

Shortly after that event, we hired a book jacket designer and gave him the words: *Make Karma Your Niche: How Relationship Marketing Attracts Massive Results in Business and in Life.*

My team and I were excited about the title. It kind of said it all. The definition of "niche" is to specialize in something. So if you "make karma your niche," then you are specializing in using karma to attract success. Because of this, I refer to making karma your niche numerous times throughout this book.

It's obvious that we ended up not using this as the title and here's why. Thirty days prior to my rough draft deadline I was giving a keynote speech at my company's annual convention. We had a rough draft completed on the jacket design of the book and I wanted to announce that the book would soon be released.

When I was wrapping up my speech, I needed to show the audience the book and announce our next speaker, Dr. Ivan Misner, who also had a bestselling business book he was currently selling. I showed them the cover of my book and told them when it would be released. I then showed them the cover of his book next to mine:

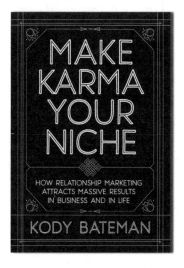 

I could see this image on the prompter in front of the stage. It was like a brick hit me right upside my head. I instantly noticed that my book design did not convey a business feel at all. In fact, it looked more like a new age philosophy book.

When I got off stage I called my editor and told her my concerns. She said, "It's funny you bring this up because the cover designer has the same concerns." It turns out that no matter what design they came up with, the word karma took away from a business feel. So at the bottom of the twelfth hour we changed the title and subtitle to what you see on the cover.

Now why do you suppose I shared this story with you as part of this introduction? Ironically, it represents the essence of my ongoing challenge. Karma is the key to success in relationship marketing and in life. But we live in a world that doesn't resonate with that message. We have been taught that systems, statistics and logic are what drive business. Karma and the simple principles of the laws of attraction don't seem to fit in; they don't appear to be sophisticated enough.

I have a company that offers the best relationship marketing system in the world today, but it has to be driven by the heart. I spend most of my time teaching people this important principle. People want to know the "how" before they want to know the "why." If you are in business and want to improve your business, you want the teacher or writer to cut to the chase. You want the list of "how-to's" and you want to hurry the process and attempt the list we give you.

I have seen so many people attempt to incorporate relationship marketing by going through the motions. They are focused on the business side of it. They are focused on what they can *get* from the activity, not on what they can *give* to it. Relationship marketing is about relationships, not about marketing. Most people have this turned around.

The business books give you the "how-to" lists. This book does as well. The new age personal development books give you the philosophy and vision that should drive what you do. This book does that as well. The two book designs represent what is needed to succeed. The business "how to" coupled with the true philosophy of "why" is wrapped up in *The Power of Human Connection*. You want to know how relationship marketing can transform the way you succeed in business and in life. That's why those words are on the cover of this book. The way you truly master relationship marketing is through genuine human connection. That's why you see that as the title of this book.

I will be referring to human connection and to making karma your niche throughout these pages. Why? Because your niche is what you specialize in. If you specialize in leveraging karma or "making karma your niche," then you will naturally get better at generating genuine human connection. That, my friends, is critical, because human connection is what it takes to get the best results with your relationship marketing activities.

In this book, I'm going to leverage what you want from me, which is a way for you to increase sales and profits in your business. I'm going to inspire you on what you need from me, which is to focus on genuine connection, create quality relationships, and truly care about people in your life. You see, the things you need will generate the things you want.

Chances are, there is an example or story in this book that is directly tied to your chosen business niche. You will learn specifically the best practices to leverage relationship marketing to your benefit. We have seen amazing results in real estate, insurance, car dealerships, corporate sales, various retail niches, health care, home builders, tree services, car repair, direct sales—and the list goes on and on.

The Power of Human Connection is an exploration into the profound benefits of positivity and appreciation. You will enjoy these benefits when you make karma your niche or specialty. Your quality of life will increase. What you appreciate will *appreciate*—meaning it will grow. If you want your relationships, your money, your business and your personal interests to grow, get bigger, get better or appreciate, then you simply appreciate those things.

To get us started, I'm going to jump right into the true meaning of relationship marketing. What you want from me is the second word: marketing. What you need from me is the first word: relationship. That is the very conversation that will teach you what relationship marketing really is and how you can leverage it to its full potential. Turn to the first chapter and let's go to work.

SECTION 1

WHAT RELATIONSHIP MARKETING REALLY IS

CHAPTER 1

Relationship Marketing Overview

When most people in business see the term "relationship marketing," they focus on the second word over the first. They want to know how it will benefit them or what they will get out of it. Others will teach that relationship marketing is about mining your database, analyzing customer activity and then targeting key opportunities to drip on your customer to generate more sales and referrals.

Though the activities are accurate and part of a good relationship marketing program, they should never be the primary focus. If that is the primary focus you will get moderate results. This book and its philosophy are not interested in moderate results.

I will show you how to get massive results with a solid relationship marketing plan. But I need to begin by rewiring your mind on what relationship marketing actually is.

There is a reason the word relationship comes first. Relationship must be the primary focus—not marketing. There are lots of sales and marketing trainers who may want to debate that, but the business world is beginning to realize everything in life is about creating relationships. Everything.

If you want to make karma your niche or your specialty, you need to master relationships in three core areas: relationships with your **self**, relationships that are **personal**, and relationships in **business**.

To do this, you simply find out who you are (this is relationship with **self**) and then give yourself away to people in your **personal** and **business** life. In creating relationship with **self**, you establish who you are, what you have to contribute, what makes you unique, and pinpoint your unique selling proposition.

Again, find out who you are and then give yourself away to people in your personal life and in your business. People ask me all the time what I mean by this. Again, it's simple: treat others, in all walks of life, the way you want to be treated. Be giving, caring and humble, especially to those who cannot currently offer you anything in return. Being nice to people is not something you should turn on and off. Being nice should become who you are as a person.

At the end of the day people don't buy your products, your services, your offers or your gimmicks. They buy you. The best way to establish relationship is to be kind, caring, and giving, and to take a personal interest in others every day.

In his book *Way of the Wolf*, Jordan Belfort talks about three things your prospects must feel at a high level before they will purchase from you. They must:

1. Love your product.
2. Trust and connect with you.
3. Trust and connect with your company.

Usually the biggest issue that blocks the sale is the second item, trusting and connecting with you, Belfort says. By focusing on the three core relationship areas you will build trust and connection with people you seek to do business with. After all, people buy from those they know, like, and trust.

Along with three core relationship areas, **self**, **personal** and **business**, there are three core principles to a strong relationship marketing plan:

Core Principle #1
Define your personal brand and build it with:
· **Friendship**
· **Celebration**
· **Service**

This simply means you represent who you are in your personal brand and then you create friendship by celebrating your prospects and customers with appreciation. Thank you, birthday, holiday, keep in touch, and lifestyle celebration are key opportunities to do this. You also provide impeccable service. What's interesting is that when you focus on establishing relationship in this fashion, you naturally want to raise the bar on how well you take care of your prospect or customer.

Core Principle #2
Focus on relationship 80 percent of the time and marketing 20 percent of the time.

This simply means when you reach out to your prospects and customers, the primary focus is relationship. Again, you have key opportunities to do this. When you say thank you, only say thank you. When you celebrate a birthday, only say happy birthday. Same thing with holidays, staying in touch, and lifestyle celebrations. I have often said, "Don't ask for the referral: deserve it."

This chart illustrates the 80/20 principle in action.

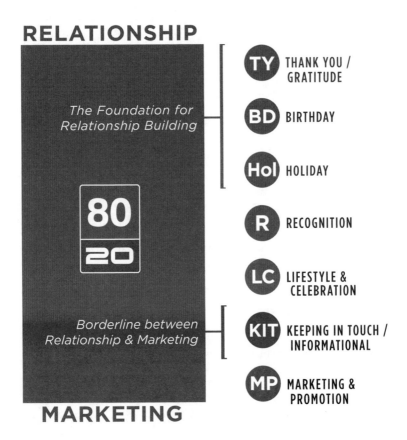

Core Principle #3
Bridge the gap between high-tech and personal touch.

Our marketing programs focus on the tangible touch: a real physical greeting card and sometimes a gift that physically shows up in the mailbox. This is critical to an effective relationship marketing plan. Email, social media, and other digital forms of communication have become the mainstream method of dripping on your prospects and customers. Remember when email was a brand new phenomenon, back in the "You've got mail!" era? Well now the tide has almost completely shifted back to the physical mailbox.

There are massive amounts of data competing with your message when you use social media, and your digital inbox is now cluttered with inbound messaging that is annoying; it's simple to get lost in the clutter. Only 11 percent of emails ever get opened, let alone read. Remember, if it is easy and cheap, everyone will do it. I want to be clear. I'm not saying that digital communication is bad. I believe it is essential as part of your communication arsenal. But using a tangible touch with a printed card sent in the mail will separate you from the clutter. It will show you care.

Even if you don't care that much about the human being who is behind the title of customer or prospect, you will start caring after sending a few heartfelt cards. It's like my mentor and dear friend the late Perry Kassing used to say, "Pretend that you like someone and pretty soon you will." You will begin to make connection in your own mind and then the connection will grow with others.

A greeting card is 11 times more likely to be opened than any other piece of mail, and the tangible thank you card generates more referral business than any other form of communication. Can you believe fewer than 3 percent of businesspeople send a thank you card? Their oversight is your opportunity.

There is technology available today that allows you to keep track of and send customized cards and gifts with pictures, custom messages, even in your own handwriting, if you choose. And you can do it from the convenience of your smartphone or computer. This is bridging the gap between high-tech and personal touch, and it is essential for you to incorporate this if you wish to remain competitive in our Google-based world.

Think about it. If someone wants your product or service, they can Google you and your competition in seconds. They can find out what you and your competitor are offering before you even talk to them. This is why personal relationship is becoming more and more important in today's world. People could care less about how much you know, especially today. People only care about how much you care. All marketing is transactional; you set yourself apart by reaching out in kindness and purely with the intent to stay in touch with your customers.

I personally experienced the power of these principles in a recent interaction that was a potential buying transaction. I recently purchased a new Dodge 4x4 mega cab truck. It is a beautiful truck that does everything I need it to do, and I've optioned it up just the way I like it. It is the first Dodge I have ever owned. I have been a Ford guy my whole life. I had a 2011 crew cab diesel Ford that began to give me problems, twice blowing the turbo out when I was pulling a heavy trailer to and from my cabin. After the second time, I got ticked off and decided to dump it for a new truck. My next-door neighbor referred me to a salesperson at the

Dodge dealership, and I ended up trading in the Ford truck for a new Dodge.

Shortly after I did this, Ford came out with a new body style turbo diesel truck. I love the looks and performance of the new Ford truck, and my research showed it was the superior truck on the market. My Dodge only had 26,000 miles on it and it still had its first set of tires, but I decided I still wanted to look into buying a new Ford. When I was ready to call someone about looking into a new truck, I realized I had nobody to call. I have purchased six new Ford trucks in the past 20 years—but I had nobody to call. I'm in the relationship marketing business, so it's been clear to me for years that dealerships have a challenge with follow-up, and that's likely due to a high turnover. But still, no one had bothered to keep in touch with me—a guy who buys a lot of vehicles.

To be fair, dealerships typically want to create the relationship directly with their buyers because in general, salespeople at dealerships only last about 90 to 120 days. So if the only person I've dealt with in the past has moved on—also without telling me where he/she moved on to—I don't have a relationship to rely on. But in general, I feel it's safe to say dealerships do a terrible job maintaining a relationship with their customers, although they do send out form letters from time to time asking their customers to fill out surveys. That doesn't do a lot for the personal relationship, does it?

So here is what happened. I simply went back to the last guy I bought a truck from—the Dodge guy. I had to contact my neighbor to get his phone number because, you guessed it, the salesman never followed up with me after I purchased the Dodge truck. I contacted him and found out his dealership was part of an auto group that also had a Ford dealership. He referred me to one of his associates who worked at the Ford store. So I went down and met with the guy. Keep in mind, I wasn't highly motivated to purchase because I already had a new truck fixed up the way I like it. I told him the numbers I needed in order to make the deal work.

He went to his sales manager, but they were about $7,500 off the deal I wanted to make. I said, "If anything changes with year-end deals or whatever, please let me know." And I drove away.

While I was there, they captured my name, phone number, email address and physical address. They had my credit score and all my personal information. Four weeks went by and I received no form of a follow-up—no thank you for coming by, not a text, no phone call—nothing. Then out of the blue I got a voicemail from the sales guy saying he has great news and to call him. I left him a text and said, "Hey thanks for getting back. If you have not shaved off the full $7,500 difference, I simply don't have the motivation to buy." And again—nothing.

Another four weeks went by and I heard nothing. I guess that meant they didn't have the deal I needed, or maybe they were too busy to deal with a paying customer, or they simply didn't care. Who knows? Then again out of the blue I get another voicemail from the salesman, saying he thinks he can get really close to the deal I asked for. What do you think I did? You guessed it: absolutely nothing.

There is one thing I can guarantee you. At any time during this eight-week process, if I had received a simple thank you text or card in the mail from the sales guy or his sales manager (or better yet, both), there is no doubt I would be driving a new Ford right now. And it doesn't stop there. Three of my closest friends want to buy the new Ford, and I guarantee I would have referred them there.

This kind of stuff drives me crazy. I have a passion to teach the business world to wake up and do some simple things to show that you care about people. These aren't just transactions and potential commissions walking through your door or lighting up your phone; these are people. And there is no better way to build your book of business than by building solid relationships. Showing people you care is not rocket science, nor is it time-consuming.

One guy who really took this to a whole new level is Joe Girard, a car salesman who is in the *Guinness Book of World Records* for selling the most cars in a year—1,475 cars, in the year 1973. Over a 15-year period in the car business, he sold a record 13,001 cars. He did not own the dealership and he didn't have fleet sales as part of this number. How did he do it? Simple. He connected with his customers, asked about their birthdays, their families, and then sent greeting cards, starting with the thank you card and birthday cards, several times throughout the year. Do you think he stayed top of mind with his customers? You bet he did.

This is neither difficult nor is it time-consuming. That which you appreciate, appreciates. Why salespeople don't understand this is beyond me. I like to see people succeed, so it's my passion to change that.

If you make it a conscious process to focus on relationship with **self**, with **others**, and with **business**, you will make the necessary shifts to master relationship marketing. The key to doing this is to create new habits that help you master the art of building relationships.

HABITS FOR MASTERING RELATIONSHIP WITH SELF:

- Nourish yourself with positivity every day.
- Read positive books.
- Listen to positive recordings.
- Send positivity to others (**send heartfelt greeting cards**).
- Never go to bed after watching the news.
- Always read or listen to positivity right before sleeping.
- Keep a journal.
- Know your "why" and write "I am" statements.
- Set specific goals.

Remember, you are finding out and nourishing who you are so you can give yourself away.

HABITS FOR MASTERING RELATIONSHIP WITH OTHERS:

- Always smile at others, everywhere you go.
- Say hello to people and express positive greetings.
- Open doors, give people the parking space, and let people in when you're in traffic.
- Always be pleasant; you never know who you are talking to.
- Say please and thank you.
- Listen more than you speak.
- Be nice to people.
- Celebrate people with pictures, gifts and your written words (**send heartfelt greeting cards**).

• Share compliments and appreciation daily.

Some of the things on this list may seem trivial and unrelated to relationship marketing, but I assure you they are essential. Good habits like this will help you be in the right mindset when you establish relationships and business dealings with other people.

The ideal mindset for mastering relationships is this: "The world and the people in it owe you nothing. But you owe it to yourself to give the world and the people in it everything. So find out who you are and then give yourself away." Creating these habits will help you do this.

HABITS FOR MASTERING RELATIONSHIPS IN BUSINESS:

• Make a list of everyone you know and put them in a contact manager of your choice. Create three primary categories: 1) contacts, 2) prospects, 3) customers. Always add people to your list and move them through the three categories.

• Take detailed notes on all your contacts.

• Reach out in the spirit of **relationship** 80 percent of the time and the spirit of **marketing** 20 percent of the time.

• Build your personal brand with friendship, celebration and service.

• Use the four methods of communication to reach out regularly to your lists. The four methods are:

Text

Call

Greeting cards **(send heartfelt greeting cards)**

Electronic communication

Always be in the spirit of service. Give for the sake of giving, and you will attract what you give. Listen more than you speak and always make it about them and how you can help them. It is not enough to know and memorize this list; it's not even enough to implement this list. You need to make this list and the methods of communication your habits.

You know a habit is formed when you no longer think about the activity—you just do it. Here is a list of habits most people have:

Brushing your teeth

Tying your shoes

Taking a shower

Driving your car

Scrolling on social media (I wish I didn't have to use this one)

You get the idea. Think about each of those activities. You are on autopilot when you do them.

Several studies have determined there are four levels to creating a habit, good or bad, in your life.

Level 1: Unconscious incompetence. This is where you don't think about it and don't do it.

Level 2: Conscious incompetence. This is where you think about it but don't do it.

Level 3: Conscious competence. This is where you think about it and then you do it.

Level 4: Unconscious competence. This is where you no longer think about it, you just do it. Level 4 is when it becomes a habit.

To master anything, it's not enough to know or even do the list of fundamentals. You need to make them habits. This is why it's really important to understand how a habit is created.

I would like you to do a quick activity. Following this paragraph are three sets of infinity signs. You will notice they each have a center point with an arrow pointed downward and to the left. Take a pen and point it in the center of the first infinity sign. Then sketch in the direction of the arrow and follow the lines until you make it around once and you are back at the center point.

Now take your pen and point it in the center of the second infinity sign below. Then sketch in the direction of the arrow and follow the lines until you make it around three times and rest at the center point.

Now take your pen and point it in the center of the third infinity sign on the next page. Then sketch in the direction of the arrow and follow the lines. This time, I want you to freely sketch for at least 20 seconds and then rest at the center point.

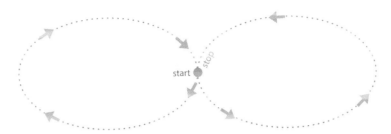

What did you notice about this activity? The first time when you only sketched once, it was probably a bit awkward. You were thinking about it and doing it (conscious competence). The second time when you sketched three times, it was probably still a bit awkward, but became a little easier as you went. Notice that for part of this activity, you had to count the number of times you made it around (three times). You were still thinking about it and doing it (conscious competence). The third time, when you sketched freely, it should have gotten easier and easier. In fact, within the 20 seconds, you probably got to where you were not thinking about it—you were just doing it (unconscious competence).

Let's go back to the goal of relationship mastery in the three core areas: **self**, **others** and **business**. Study those lists and start to do them until they become habit. You will notice there is one activity that's listed in each of the three core areas. I did this for emphasis. Each time I put that activity in parenthesis and bolded the letters: **Send heartfelt greeting cards.**

I did this because that's how important this activity is. I have learned that one of the greatest activities to generate positivity and positive laws of attraction in your life is to send out positivity in the spirit of celebration and appreciation. This is even stronger than reading and listening. What you send out in life is what comes back to you. Sending real greeting cards, where you can express yourself with the written word, is perhaps the best way to do this.

This is a great way to nourish your relationship with **self** on a daily basis. Then, in sending those cards, you nourish your relationships with **others** in your personal life. And, of course, you nourish relationships with people in your **business**.

What the marketplace wants is the last one—improve relationships in **business** so you can get more business. What the marketplace needs is all three, with emphasis on the first two: **self** and **others**. And when you master the first two, the third one, **business**, takes care of itself.

You will also notice if you master genuine heartfelt card-sending, it will take care of many of the other items on the list. I don't need to spell that out for you. You can easily figure that out on your own if you study the three lists and see how many items are touched simply by sending greeting cards.

It takes time, patience and commitment to become a master at anything. If you make these things your daily habits and have a system you can use to keep you on track, you will master relationship marketing and set yourself apart from others.

The key to this is found in one single word: consistency. Consistent effort over time is what turns activities into a habit. Consistency with the right activities will win over talent, connections, ability, or education. Successful people are habitually consistent with the right activities.

Most people in sales say to sell the sizzle and not the steak. Many writers and trainers do the same thing. You have to read 30 or 40 pages of sizzle before you get to the steak. I gave you the steak up front. The very first chapter outlines most of the components in a good relationship marketing plan. The rest of the chapters will go into detail on these components. You will read stories of real people implementing these components and learn about the massive results they get.

Leveraging a relationship marketing system that sends the right communication touches at the right times will generate referral business and incremental sales. What you need is a way to express your heart and make genuine connection with other human beings.

You want the system. You need the heart. Let's explore this balance next.

CHAPTER 2

Balance Between System and Heart

n late fall, 2002, I was asked for the second straight year to speak at the Malibu Boat dealer show in Austin, Texas. They wanted me to talk about our relationship marketing system and how it could help their boat dealers follow up with their customers.

The previous year, I'd spoken for 30 minutes and showed a fancy PowerPoint where I outlined our program, showed them examples, and then asked them to see us at our booth. In that speech I focused on the system. After all, that's what they wanted from me—to show a system. After the speech, seven or eight dealerships came to our booth to learn more about our program. It was a moderately successful show for us.

So the second year I showed up with a similar presentation. But it just so happened that this event fell on my daughter's fifteenth birthday, and for the first time in my daughter's life, I was not going to be with her on her birthday. I was feeling bad about it, and wanted to do something she would always remember.

As I began, I told the audience I had a prepared presentation similar to what I had presented the year before. "But I'm not going to share that with you today," I said. "It's my daughter's birthday tomorrow, and for the first time in her 15 years, I am not going to be home for her birthday. So I'm going to send my daughter a birthday card and you are going to help me do it."

At the time, my daughter was on her high school drill team, so I put a picture of her dancing at a team performance up on the screen. I told the group I was going to put that picture on the front of a greeting card, showing them the process as I completed it. "Now I'm going to write a message on the inside to my daughter," I said. Somewhat jokingly, I asked, "What should I say?" Many of them started yelling out things I should include in my message.

Keep in mind, I built this card right in front of them. I was showing them how our system would allow them to do that. But it wasn't the system that got their attention. It was the affection I felt for my daughter. They experienced the story with me and they loved it.

Dear Whitney,

I am sending you this card from Austin Texas, in front of 200 Malibu boat dealers. I am feeling bad that I am not home for your birthday. So from me and all of these dealers, we wish you a Happy Birthday.

Love you sweetheart,

Your Dad

That was it. I was done. After showing the card I said, "I'm not going to show the rest of my slides today. I just want you to know that you can do the same thing with your family and personal friends, and you can do it with your new boat buyers. If you want to know more, come on back and we will help you." And then I went back to my booth. Even though I had a 30-minute time slot for this presentation, I was done in seven minutes.

This time we were flooded at our booth. We had people from more than 30 dealerships who wanted to know how they could do what I had just showed them.

So what was the difference between the first year and the second year? The first year I showed the system. The second year I showed the heart. What the marketplace wants from me is a system, but what they need is the heart. That story took place over 15 years ago. We have been teaching people our system and our philosophy ever since.

....

One thing I've found is that until people
find the heart in what they are sending, they
never seem to get around to sending. But
I've also found if I can get people to use this
system in their personal life—sending cards to
loved ones—then they will send them more
consistently in their business.

....

They will also be more personal with the messages to people they do business with. This is the key to getting massive results versus mediocre results with a relationship marketing plan. Again, it's all about making connection, and the best way to do that is to show people you care.

Let's have a little fun right now. Let's go back to the habit formation exercise we did in the last chapter, but this time, we are going to put the word "system" in the left side of the infinity sign and the word "heart" in the right side of the infinity sign. Now I want you to freely sketch for about 20 seconds. Make sure you take note of the words you are sketching around.

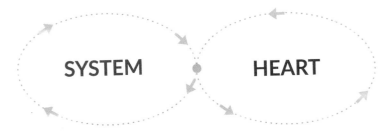

Make it a habit to maintain a balance between the system and the heart of your relationship marketing activities. One of the best ways to do that is to send "lifestyle celebration" cards to people you meet or who are already in your list of contacts. My dear friend Gayle Zientek tells an amazing story about her experience with this activity:

In March of 2011, we attended a networking event called The Taste of the Chamber. There were 20 executive chefs serving their best dishes. Over 300 networkers tasted the food and voted for their favorite. At the end of the day, the Park Street Market was crowned champion.

I had developed a habit of taking pictures and carried my Canon SureShot camera everywhere. I captured the silver platter recognition at the Taste of the Chamber, knowing I would celebrate this moment with a personalized card. I took a business card from the table to secure an address for the card. When I returned home that evening, I uploaded the pictures, created a card and clicked the "send" button on my computer.

The card said, "Your food rocked the house at the Taste of the Chamber. No better ribs, greens, or peach cobbler. A win well earned! Thanks for sharing your goodness. We enjoyed every bite. Live Today. Enjoy Life!

Then we signed it, Steve and Gayle Zientek, The Network Team, and included our phone numbers.

About a week later, I received a phone call. It was Kiar Gamsho. He thanked me for the card. He also mentioned that he and his family were relocating from the east side of the state. They would be looking to purchase homes and asked if we could meet to see if we'd be a good fit to work together. We met downtown and had a great conversation.

We kept in contact over the next year, occasionally looking at homes. In late 2012, Kiar closed on his first home. In April 2013 we were invited to Kiar and Eva's wedding. It was one of the most incredible weddings we've ever attended. We met the family and danced the night away. Over the next five years, we helped nine family members and friends buy and sell homes, earning more than $70,000 in commissions.

More importantly, we have created a special bond with the Gamsho family. They text us pictures of their new babies, invite us to dinner and tell us often how much they love us. It's been quite a journey with this family so far.

One unexpected card sent in celebration of a win well-earned led us to significant income and priceless friendships.

The reason Gayle has this story to tell is because she and her husband Steve have developed a level-four habit of sending cards. They don't think about it—they just do it. They committed to a daily routine looking for opportunities to celebrate their relationships with cards and gifts. They send an average of three to four cards every day. This consistent action helped them grow their referral business from 35 percent to 100 percent during the dismal real estate market from 2008 to 2011.

The amazing thing about this story is that Gayle did not send this card with the intention of getting anything from Kiar. She simply celebrated someone she met who won a cooking contest at a networking event.

We call this "giving to give." Most people interact with others, especially in business, with the intent to get something from them. The simple law of attraction dictates that whatever you send out will come back to you.

If you are sending messages out to give, then the universe or the people in it will give back to you. If you are sending out to get, then the universe or the people in it will get or take away. The attitude of giving is usually delivered in the form of appreciation or celebration. The attitude of getting is usually delivered in the form of a sales pitch or a persuasion.

Which of these two things do you want to receive from others in your personal life or in your business dealings? Which of these two will you give back? Gayle's story is an amazing example of this principle in action.

Here is an example of a State Farm insurance agent who, with the help of his parent company, was sending out to get something from his customers. One of his form letters found its way in the mailbox of my good friend Steve Schulz. It just so happens that Steve is a master at relationship marketing, so he set out to help this guy correct his approach. Here is Steve's story:

Have you ever received a letter like this?

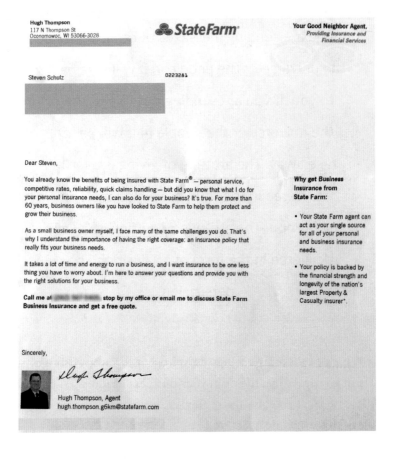

I know for a fact that my State Farm agent did not send me this letter. I have known him for over 25 years. Our children went to school together. We coached basketball together. We see each other at the YMCA almost every day. He would never personally send me an informal form letter like this.

When I received this letter I decided to have a little fun. I took the letter down to his office and I threw it on his desk.

I asked him jokingly, "Did you send me this letter?" He replied, "No."

I pointed to the picture of him on the bottom of the letter and said, "That's not you?" He laughed and said, "Yes that's me, but corporate sends out these letters."

I said, "You obviously must know when corporate is going to send out these letters. I'm guessing you need to get some temporary help in the office to answer phones and to help write policies because when people go to their mailbox and see the letter from State Farm, I'm sure they get all excited and rush down to your office and you write them a policy. Correct?"

Grinning, he replied, "No!"

I asked him, in the 32 years that he has been selling insurance, how many policies had he written off a letter like this? His response was not surprising. His answer was none. Not one single policy! I asked him again, "Then why do you send out the letter?" He said, "I don't, corporate does."

I went on to show him the real power of building relationships. This is what he now sends to his customers and clients:

This is a greeting card he sent to one of his customers
who coaches an eighth-grade girls select basketball team.
The card simply says on the front, Full of Gratitude. There's
a picture of the girls on the front of the card as well. On
the inside, it simply says, "Jerry, congratulations on winning
the championship this past weekend. The girls played great.
Make sure you share! Well done! Talk soon, Hugh."

The reason Hugh said in the card, "Make sure you share,"
is because he sent 36 brownies along with the card to celebrate the girls' championship.

What makes this card so amazing is there is nothing about
State Farm anywhere on the card. Hugh is doing nothing
except building a relationship. He is not asking anything of
Jerry. He is simply celebrating Jerry's life and his great accomplishment. He understands the importance of building

relationships 80 percent of the time and marketing 20 percent of the time.

What can we learn from this simple example? The form letter sent by Hugh's corporate office was an example of "sending out to get," and it came from a form system. The celebration greeting card sent by Hugh was "sending out to give," and it came from the heart. Yes, there was also a system that helped him build and send the card, but it was the heart—showing that he cared—that made the connection. The 36 brownies probably helped as well.

Since doing this, Hugh's referral business has skyrocketed. Again, when you are "sending to give" then the universe gives back.

In this chapter I showed you three examples of lifestyle celebration cards. The first one was a birthday card to my daughter that celebrated her love of dancing. The second one was a congratulations card celebrating a chef who won a cooking competition. The third one was a congratulations card where Hugh, the insurance guy, was celebrating the basketball victory of one of his client's children.

In all three cases, each of the people sending the cards had this in common: they are habitual card senders, and they send cards to personal friends and family as well as to business associates.

What I have found is the more people send heartfelt cards, the more clouded the line gets between personal and business relationships. It's no longer about the type of relationship you have with someone; it's all about the simple celebration of people in your life. When you get to this level, you can master relationship marketing and achieve massive results in your business and personal life.

Creating genuine human connection is about becoming a specialist in sending positivity out to the world. It's about celebrating other people and sharing appreciation consistently. It's about making connections with real people using a combination of digital and tangible communication, including texting, email, social media, phone calls, face-to-face interactions, and greeting cards.

Most importantly, if you want to be on the good side of karma, you need to master the balance between having a system to use and a heart to use it with. You just experienced some remarkable stories about the heart. All the examples came from using a system, but you heard about the heart that went into the system.

CHAPTER 3

Relationship Marketing System

Make no mistake, the system is about generating sales and profits. As an entrepreneur, I am about generating sales and profits. I like to make money and you should as well.

As my mentor the late Zig Ziglar used to say, "Money is not the most important thing in the world but it ranks right up there with oxygen." I have also heard this said: "The person who thinks money is a bad thing doesn't have enough of it."

So let's talk about having a system that generates sales and profits. The second principle in our relationship marketing system is to focus on relationship 80 percent of the time and marketing 20 percent of the time. This chapter is about the 20 percent:

- Mining your customer base
- Creating prospects
- Delivering effective presentations
- Being a master at follow-up
- Generating initial sales and incremental sales
- Getting referral business
- Making money

You heard me say it. I love everything about solid marketing practices and making the sale. A lot of the time, people get the wrong impression of me as I constantly speak and train about the heartfelt, caring part of the business. I am also deeply invested in good old-fashioned marketing and sales.

Though I'm stating this chapter is about the 20 percent (marketing), you will see numerous examples of the 80 percent (relationships) in action. That is because relationships drive your results.

Earlier I mentioned Jordan Belfort, the author who wrote *Way of the Wolf*. A few years ago, a movie about him, *The Wolf of Wall Street*, was produced, with the main character played by Leonardo DiCaprio. This movie is not for the faint of heart. It was about Jordan Belfort teaching uneducated, rough-around-the-edges sales guys how to sell penny stocks to average mom-and-pop investors, and then transforming them to selling $5 stocks to the richest 1 percent of Americans. He explains this was an untapped niche in the retail stock market and no one on Wall Street had ever tried it before.

To train his colorful and unqualified crew, Belfort taught them what later became known as the Straight Line Sales System. They experienced massive success. Unfortunately, that success went to their heads and they started doing things that weren't legal. Jordan and others from that original crew ended up serving prison sentences for their violations.

When Belfort got out of prison, he was banned from selling stocks for life. He started a new career as a sales coach and speaker, teaching his Straight Line Sales system. His book *Way of the Wolf* tells behind-the-scenes stories depicted in the movie, and teaches his sales system. Like this guy or not, I have to tell you, *Way of the Wolf* is one of the best books about sales I have ever read. And I have read a lot of books about sales.

In the movie, Jordan Belfort is depicted as a ruthless salesman. In his early days, he was all about making the sale at any expense. He took it too far and the expense cost him his freedom. The reformed Belfort is still about making the sale and he is still aggressive in his approach. But he is now a much calmer, gentler, more ethical version of himself.

The polar opposite of his approach and persona is Bob Burg, author of *The Go-Giver*. His book is all about giving your way to success. He has created the go-giver concept into a successful brand and series of books. His book *Go-Givers Sell More* shows how to give your way to generating sales and profits.

I bring this up because, as luck would have it, I was reading *Way of the Wolf* and *Go-Givers Sell More* at the same time. Wow! What a contrast these two books have on generating sales.

There were times when I was saying, "C'mon Bob, there is much more to sales than just being a nice guy." And then I would say, "C'mon Jordan, quit acting like such a tough guy and realize you need to create relationships." Though both of them did talk about creating a balance between those two things, Jordan definitely represents the "close the deal" side and Bob represents the "peace and love" side of the equation.

I believe the best marketing and sales system today must represent a balance between closing the deal and creating relationships. The days of hard-line marketing and sales are over. It takes much more than a smooth-talking salesperson to close any deal today. It also takes more than just being nice. Relationships are essential to the equation.

The following chart illustrates a balance between closing the deal and creating relationships. A simplified example of traditional marketing and sales is found on the left side, while relationship marketing objectives are found on the right side. Together they create a cycle of healthy sales activity.

The left side begins with an arrow that points upward. The process of finding prospects, acquiring customers and managing those customers is an uphill effort.

You need to be at the top of your game and use the best customer relationship management (CRM) system for your business niche, use the best in inbound and outbound sales approaches, and create strong lead generation tactics, including funnel systems that filter leads properly. And you have to make sure you have state-of-the-art presentation capabilities and follow-up systems.

The right side begins with an arrow that points downward. A solid relationship marketing effort is all about building relationships. Those relationships naturally transform into developing new customers, retaining existing customers, and generating new business from referrals. This is a downhill effort.

Imagine being a cyclist. You have a challenging incline where you are pedaling uphill for about 10 miles. When you reach the summit, you begin your downhill stretch for another 10 miles. You're able to coast, occasionally pedal, and enjoy a fun ride. This is what it's like to create a balance between your traditional marketing and sales and your relationship marketing efforts.

You will notice the chart represents a cycle. Your relationship marketing efforts rejuvenate your sales efforts. If done correctly, the ride gets easier and easier. It's like the uphill stretches are more sporadic. You have speed and momentum coming out of your downhill so it's easier to pedal up the next incline.

Gayle Zientek, the real estate broker I mentioned earlier, increased her referral business from 35 percent to 100 percent within two years. She did this with a solid relationship marketing plan that utilized social media and greeting cards.

Think about it. If 100 percent of your leads are coming from referrals, how much easier will the ride be? The referral gives you momentum as you ride into the uphill side of your marketing and sales efforts. It's like you coasted right through the "finding prospects" part of the incline because the referral is the prospect. You still have to do some pedaling. You need to take care of that referral with solid sales and service tactics. You need to convert that referral into a customer and take good care of them. I'm sure you've heard the saying, "It costs far less to retain a customer than it does to find a new one." No truer words have ever been spoken.

If done correctly, the right side of this chart is far more cost-efficient than the left side. The average cost ratio is about 10 to one. So for every $1,000 spent in traditional sales and marketing, you can get the same return for $100 invested with the right relationship marketing program.

Those efficiencies will only increase as we move forward in today's marketplace, and here's why. We live in a Google and social media world, where traditional marketing is less effective because people have access to more information. They also receive immediate feedback from other consumers who may be purchasing from you or your competitors. Because of this, positive relationships in today's business world are more important than ever. Digital communication is not enough. In fact, in many cases, it's more of a turnoff because email and all the forms of social media are being done by everyone. We are bombarded with digital forms of communication, and most of it is traditional marketing.

Anything you can do to impress your customers and help them feel appreciated will set you apart and create the word-of-mouth or referral business that's essential in today's marketplace. As the whole business world communicates digitally, you can make the extra effort by sending something physical to your customers and prospects.

I have spent the past 20 years developing education and systems that help businesses around the world deliver the perfect relationship marketing plan. You can see what I've built at www.kodybateman.com, where you can have free access to thousands of recorded interviews and articles on this subject. You can also go to www.sendoutcards.com for the premier, stand-alone relationship marketing system and to www.sendogo.com for the premier integration system that works right inside your CRM of choice. Those services provide the world's best systems for delivering tangible touches complete with greeting cards and gift impressions. And you can do it right from the convenience of your computer or smartphone. We make it as simple as sending a digital message. This is true relationship marketing at its very best.

Since relationship marketing is so important, we need to take a closer look at the right side of the sales cycle. The best way to build relationships, develop and retain customers, and generate referrals is to implement the r80/m20 rule—**r80** stands for relationships 80 percent of the time and **m20** stands for marketing 20 percent of the time. That is the second core principle of our relationship marketing philosophy. The right side of the following chart shows the ideal opportunities to reach out to prospects and customers.

Good relationship marketing campaigns are built around the (TY) thank you, (B) birthday, and (H) holiday touches. I call this the hub. You can add anniversary, lifestyle celebration, keep in touch, and specific marketing touches, as the chart below illustrates.

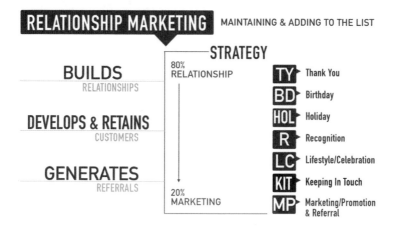

You certainly don't have to use all of these, with the exception of the thank you card. As you will soon find out, the thank you card is critical. It's the most powerful touch you can send, bar none. If you do nothing more than master the thank you card, you will have massive success.

Another powerful single touch impression is the lifestyle celebration card, where you celebrate peoples' accomplishments by sending them a card. You have already read examples of this with Gayle Zientek sending the Taste of the Chamber congratulations card, and Hugh, the State Farm agent, who congratulated the local girls' basketball team.

What you see in blue on the chart on the previous page represents the relationship touches, purple can be a hybrid between relationship and marketing, and pink is a marketing touch. You can visually see the r80/m20 rule represented with the type of touch this calls for. Let's face it: most businesspeople who are tasked to generate revenue focus on the marketing and sales side far more than they focus on relationships. The reason is they don't know what I just showed you.

Because of this, it is necessary to teach the philosophy and provide a way for businesspeople to implement relationship marketing to their advantage. We provide the training and the systems that will help you do just that.

THE POWER OF THE THANK YOU CARD

This is the single most important impression you can place on someone in your business dealings and in your personal life. Again, an email, text, social post, or even a form letter is not enough. In fact, in some cases they might be worse than doing nothing at all.

The golden test is to simply think of how you feel when a company or individual you have done business with does or doesn't thank you and stay in touch with you. Think about how you feel when:

- You receive nothing.
- You receive an email thanking you for your business but also asking you for more business.
- You receive a thank you email asking you to fill out a survey.
- You receive an impersonal form letter thanking you and asking you to do something.

The majority of this type of attempt is usually auto-triggered from a company's CRM. It has a corporate form feel to it, and it's plastered with company branding. They typically give you the feeling that they want to get more out of you, not that they want to give you a genuine message of gratitude.

Here are some examples of mail we all receive and quickly find a trash button or trash can for.

Let's compare that approach to a true relationship marketing effort. First of all, a greeting card is 11 times more likely to get opened than any other piece of mail. The average email open rate has dwindled to around 11 percent.

A greeting card that is printed on high quality paper, and personalized with pictures, personal handwriting, and personal branding, shows you care enough to go above and beyond. It leaves a lasting impression on those who receive it.

This example was an actual card I sent after attending an investment opportunity meeting. While I was there, I took a photo of the gentlemen I met with, went to my car after the meeting, pulled up an app on my smartphone, and sent this card in under a minute.

Here is what's interesting about this story. The gentlemen you see in this picture invited me to look at an investment opportunity. They wanted me to give them money. Do you think I received a thank you card from any of them? That's not hard to figure out. The answer is no. Over 90 percent of salespeople never send a thank you card.

Why do you suppose I sent them a thank you card? Because it's a habit for me to send greeting cards, especially thank you cards. I can't turn that off. It doesn't matter if I'm selling or being sold to, I send the cards out.

I always suggest that you personalize your thank you impression with a picture of the person you are sending the card to, a personalized message, and a signature with your printed name and phone number underneath the signature. This keeps you top of mind with the person you send the card to, and also makes it convenient for them to contact you if they need to.

The initial business transaction is usually about meeting to explore the possibilities of doing business together. I suggest having thank you, nice to meet you and celebrating new possibilities card designs pre-saved and ready to send out with the ease described in this example. I also suggest you personally brand the back of these cards as you see in the examples below.

I could have used any of those headlines to follow up with my investment meeting.

You can also conveniently add specialty gift items to go with your cards. This further enhances the impression you leave on the person you are reaching out to.

We highly recommend anyone doing business have a personalized approach like this to make a lasting first impression. Again, if the single-impression thank you approach was the only thing you added to your traditional marketing and sales practices, you would dramatically improve your results.

I love sharing the story of Dave Potter. He owns a tree service in Port Alberni, British Columbia, Canada. I had the opportunity to interview Dave on my *Relationship Marketing Weekly* show. What a riot. This guy was on the job in a bucket about 50 feet off the ground. He had all his gear on and he was pruning trees high above the ground when our show started.

So the first thing I asked him was, "How much time do you spend off the ground in that bucket?" He laughed and said, "I'm either in the bucket or sharpening saws." He and his crew are very busy every day.

Keep in mind, he was on my show to explain how he follows up with his customers. So, I asked him, "When do you possibly have time to follow up with your customers when you're up in the tree all the time?"

He then showed us exactly what he does. He pulled his smartphone out of his pocket and said, "I carry this thing with me everywhere I go and I take pictures. It's important to me to get cool pictures on the job. I get pictures of my customers, of their property, and of the progress we make as we do the job. When I'm up here in this bucket, I can get pictures of my customers' properties from an angle they have probably never seen before."

He then went on to demonstrate how he builds and sends them a real greeting card right from an app on his phone. Keep in mind, he is 50-plus feet off the ground in a bucket looking down at his customer's property. He took a picture of that property, loaded it on the front of a card, hit the mic icon on his phone, and voiced in his message:

> "Dear Mrs. Smith,
>
> Thank you so much for the tree work. We really appreciate your business."
>
> From Dave and the Totem Crew

He then added a gift of gourmet brownies, typed in their address and hit send. Dave said it takes him two to four minutes to do this.

The most beautiful house on the street!

Gordon and Corinne
Thank you so much for the tree work today! It was a pleasure working on such a beautiful tree. Your place is absolutely amazing. Wishing you the most abundant year ever!
Dave

This guy is 50 feet up in the air in his tree service bucket, sending a thank you card and gift to his clients. To me, this shows there is really no excuse for anybody to not follow up with their customers.

Dave sends thank you cards to people he gives estimates to, thank you cards and a gift to people he did a job for, and sends Christmas cards to all his customers. After doing that for just one year, his tree service business tripled, and all of his growth came from referrals. Not once in any of his cards does he ask for a referral.

What Dave is doing is implementing the right side of the sales cycle. He is not at r80/m20; he is more like r95/m5. In fact, the only marketing he has is mentioning the name of his tree service within his message and leaving a phone number under his name. We will give him a 5 percent score on marketing for doing that.

WHAT'S EVEN BETTER THAN A THANK YOU CARD

Well, nothing is better than the thank you card, but there is something better than sending out just a single impression. Multiple-impression campaigns are highly effective because they keep you top of mind with your customers. Remember, someone who feels appreciated will appreciate your business with incremental sales and referrals.

The following is an example of a five-touch campaign that was designed for an Aston Martin dealership. The purpose of this was to show them how they could easily extend their follow-up from a single touch to five touches that would reach their customers at optimum times.

Again, the hub of a good multiple-touch campaign is built around the thank you, birthday and holiday opportunities. We simply suggested to send those and add a keep in touch and a promotional card inviting them to bring their car in for service.

In this case, the only variable piece that requires input from the salesperson is in the thank you card. They simply take a photo of the buyer next to their new car. Then they can have a pre-written thank you message already built in the card. They can overwrite that message to personalize it to that individual. Once they do that, they can click send. All four remaining impressions have pre-set photos and messages built in. This minimizes the effort but the receiver is left with the impression that the dealership went way above and beyond to make them feel appreciated.

You will notice we used the r80/m20 rule, as four out of the five impressions were strictly focused on creating relationship. The fifth impression was a marketing promotional piece inviting them to bring their car in for service. The first four messages are short, personal, and only express appreciation. The philosophy is you only say thank you, you only say happy birthday, and you only say happy holidays, with no promoting or selling of any kind.

We even recommend that any company branding be done subtly and discreetly. The more you make these impressions about the person you're sending them to or the products they are interested in, the better.

In this campaign, we recommended a keep-in-touch impression called "top-shelf living." Aston Martin owners are part of an elite club and they take great pride in their vehicles. So the keep-in-touch impression simply celebrated their car. The dealership's CRM keeps track of the exact car the buyer purchases, so when the buyer receives this impression, it can have a picture of their unique car on it.

This next example shows a motorsport dealership campaign. They did a similar five-impression campaign but used custom-built cards for each impression.

Linda Walters is a mortgage broker from Toronto Canada. She and her team send out a four-touch card campaign to everyone they do a mortgage for. The first touch is a "nice to meet you" that they send after the first meeting with a couple or family at the beginning of the tedious mortgage process. When they are done with the transaction, they send another card that says, "Thank you for the business." Their third impression is sent out on the anniversary date of their closing. The fourth impression is a keep-in-touch card that simply says they are thinking about the family and hope all is well.

Linda does not ask for referrals or promote her company's services in any way. Since incorporating this simple campaign, her mortgage company has increased its business by 71 percent, all from referral business. These phenomenal results culminated in Linda getting rid of all other advertising and marketing efforts.

Heba Malki, is co-owner of the Domilya Group, a commercial and residential construction business based in Milton, Ontario, Canada. In her first 11 years of business, she and her husband had primarily used online marketing and networking events to promote their business.

In the past three years, the couple has incorporated a strategic relationship marketing plan that has increased their revenue by 320 percent. Heba runs this program and she goes by one simple rule: everyone she meets receives a minimum of four tangible touches in the mail every year. Each multiple-touch campaign starts with a "nice to meet you" card and gift. She then sends a birthday card (if she has their birthdate), a Christmas card, Valentine's Day card, and a Happy New Year card. She does this to stay top of mind with people she meets, and her focus is to create relationships, not to generate business.

When those she meets have an interest in their construction services, she sends a "Thank you for the opportunity to bid your job" card, a "Thank you for choosing us" card, and she even sends a card when they are not chosen for the job. She then sends a thank you card and gift after completion of the job, a three-month stay in touch card, a six-month stay in touch card (usually centered around a holiday), and a 12-month stay in touch card. She even sends a thank you card to anyone who does an online review of their business.

Anyone who ends up in her marketing funnel receives at least seven cards from her company within a year. It is only after all those touches that she will send an "ask for the referral" card. She is implementing the r80/m20, and her business has received phenomenal results.

Heba tells a story about being the high bidder on one job, but how they won the job because of her card-sending habits. They were invited to bid a large renovation job for a medical office. She sent their usual "Thank you for the opportunity" card and included a box of brownies. After they completed and sent the bid, she then sent another thank you card with a large gift box.

A few days after she sent the second card and gift, they received a phone call asking them to come in for a meeting. When they got there, the first thing the doctors told them was they were the highest bidder. "We are giving you the job anyway," the doctors said. They said anyone who takes the time to follow up with the timing and class that Heba's company did must put in that kind of extra effort when doing the job. They wanted someone they could trust to finish the job right. This, my friends, is the power of human connection at its very best.

CHAPTER 4

Five Secrets to Relationship Marketing Success

The Five Secrets to Relationship Marketing Success came from numerous guests on my *Relationship Marketing Weekly* show. Each of those guests shared philosophies and activities that have made them successful. They have used relationship marketing as a way to separate themselves from their competitors. They have figured out simple ways to keep the heart at the center of their system.

THE FIRST SECRET: "THREE-LEGGED STOOL"

This concept came from Andre Perdue. He's the manager of Red Rock Collision in Tempe, Arizona. On his three-legged stool, the first leg is great service. Leg number two is communication, and leg three is appreciation.

It was fun to interview Andre because he is so passionate about the service he provides his customers. Andre is in the car collision business, so he's dealing with people who have been in car accidents. First and foremost, he says, he has to deliver impeccable service. And he has to communicate. How many of you go into repair shops or service-oriented companies and find the biggest problem is a serious lack of communication? You don't fully understand what you're getting into or what the price is. Andre makes a point to over-communicate. He says you have to spend the time massively communicating to your customer about your service, what they can expect, what they can do. "I'm going to provide the best service in the world," Andre says. "I'm going to communicate six ways until Sunday. I'm going to follow up with emails. I'm going to do all kinds of stuff to make sure you know exactly what the process is."

The third leg, appreciation, is the leg that really solidifies the three-legged stool. "If you're my customer, I'm going to appreciate you. I'm going to send out a card and gift and different things to shower you with appreciation," Andre says. "I'm not just going to share appreciation digitally. I may send an email and say thank you. But I have to follow up with a tangible touch, a card and gift in the mail. It doesn't work unless you do all three." You need to deliver impeccable service, incredible communication, and then tangible appreciation on the back end; that is how you drive your business with the heart.

THE SECOND SECRET: STAY TOP OF MIND WITH TANGIBLE TOUCHES

The tangible touch has already come up a lot in this book. But when this activity is mentioned by every guest I have had on the show, then you begin to realize just how significant it is. This is not just me pushing the use of tangible touches because I own a tangible touch delivery service. These are real businesspeople from all over the world who talk about how the tangible touch to prospects and customers has transformed their businesses.

Typically the most effective tangible touch is a greeting card and possibly a gift attached that shows up in a real mailbox. The person you are reaching out to physically opens it, feels it, smells the paper and maybe smells and tastes the gourmet food item you may have attached as a gift. There is simply no better way to stay top of mind with your network of people than this.

Paul Rising is a custom homebuilder based in Colorado Springs, Colorado. He sends out tangible touches in two different ways. The first way is the obvious one: he sends thank you cards and stay in touch cards to his prospects and clients.

The second way is less obvious but highly effective. He sends cards to celebrate people in his community. He simply follows social media and traditional community news channels to see who is doing what in the community. He tells the following story:

> There is a real estate agent we know here in Colorado Springs. We found out she had won a local award and was kind of celebrating it on Facebook. We sent her a really cool gift and a card, just saying, "Congratulations! You did a fantastic job. We appreciate you. We appreciate your contributions to the community." In turn, she called us and thanked us for that card and she said, "Hey, you know what? I have a client who's moving here from California and I would like you to meet them." So long story short, we met them and developed a little bit of a relationship. They got to see some of our products and they hired us to build their next home here in

Colorado Springs. By the way, that was a million-dollar home
order that we received from one celebration card we sent.

We have already featured this type of touch as a lifestyle celebration card. You have now seen numerous examples of this,
from the insurance agent to the real estate broker and now the
homebuilder. It keeps showing up because it works.

THE THIRD SECRET IS "THANKING PEOPLE THROUGH THE PROCESS"

Thanking people through the process simply means you thank
people through all phases of your business transaction. You always thank a prospect before you land any business with them,
you thank them for the business when the transaction is complete, and you thank them down the road, perhaps on the anniversary date of the transaction.

Both Dave Potter, the tree service guy, and Paul Rising, our
custom homebuilder, talk about the value of this. Dave always
thanks people for allowing him to do an estimate. He usually
puts a picture on a card of the property he is estimating to prune
trees. He then thanks them when the transaction is complete
with a picture of the property after he pruned the trees.

Paul Rising has a remodel division of Tara Custom Homes.
He goes out and gives bids to remodel people's homes. He does
not have their business yet, and he may never receive a dime
from those people. But he always sends them a thank you card
for giving him the time and the opportunity to place the bid. He
then thanks them when he has been chosen to do the job. He
says things like, "Thank you for choosing me. I look forward to

working with you. I am committed to doing the best job possible for you." Then he thanks them again when the job is complete by sending another card and box of brownies. Whatever line of work you are in, there is a process your prospects and customers go through with you. You can't thank people enough.

As I was writing this chapter, I took a quick break to stretch my legs, and I decided to check Facebook. The first and only post I read was from Andrea Shepherd. This is what it said:

> I'm a website designer. I specialize in websites for insurance agents. I have a few top competitors that I run up against time and time again. In most cases, my pricing is higher. I have a system in place that when I speak to someone on the phone about a website, they get a "Thank you for considering us" card and they get brownies. Every time. I don't sway from my system.
>
> This month, I talked to four prospects on the phone. All four of those folks signed on with me. Today was the fourth call. He very specifically said to me, "It was a tough choice. We were looking at you and two other firms. What it really came down to was relationships. We don't know you any better than we know them, but you stood out from the crowd with your card and brownies. You won! We figured if you hadn't even won our business yet and you sent us a card and brownies, then customer service after the fact must be equally as impressive."
>
> Thank you Kody Bateman

Can you believe that? You can't make this stuff up. So I want to say thank you to Andrea Shepherd for "Thanking through the process" and for sharing this post at the absolute perfect time.

THE FOURTH SECRET IS "YOUR BUSINESS IS ABOUT TAKING CARE OF PEOPLE"

It doesn't matter what business you're in. Everybody is in the business of taking care of people. In fact, your business is what you do; taking care of people is who you are. The better you are at taking care of people, the better your business is going to be.

You can get up every morning and decide, "I am about taking care of people who are in my life." Your business puts you in front of people. That's the opportunity you have every day to take care of somebody. So the business you do is what you do, and taking care of people is who you are.

Tom Lambert of Shadetree Automotive talks about this. He says, "We don't just fix cars. We take care of people." And everybody in his shop knows that philosophy. We don't just fix cars. We take care of people, and that makes a big difference. When you go into his automotive shop, he has freshly-baked cookies waiting for you. There's the aroma of cookies in the air and he provides that. So he is all about taking care of people and fixing cars is just a byproduct of that.

THE FIFTH SECRET IS TO "BE INTENTIONAL ABOUT RELATIONSHIPS"

Beyond Wynn is a real estate investor. He discusses the importance of being "intentional about relationships." He says if he had to make a decision between chasing money or chasing relationships, he would chase relationships every single time. He went through a monumental shift in his life to be able to say that. He went through a period of time where business was about business. It was all about making money! About 10 years into his business, he transformed into becoming a relationship person.

If you have to make a decision about pursuing money or pursuing relationships, which is it going to be? If you want relationships, you've got to be in the mindset of pursuing relationships. Get yourself out there. Talk to people. Be nice to people. Look people in the eye. Be kind to people every day. Be in it for the relationship only, not for the business that may follow. Be about people. That's what Beyond Wynn means when he says, "Be intentional about your relationships."

You simply need to care about other human beings every single day of your life. That just has to become part of you. It has to become a practice you do all the time, whether you're doing your business or not. That way, it naturally flows into your business when you're doing business.

When you are intentional about relationships, people feel that. People don't buy your product. They don't buy your service. They buy you. And so if you're intentional about your relationships, people are going to feel that and buy into you. They're going to know you truly care about them.

If you want to talk about making genuine and powerful human connections, these simple secrets will get it done. Go ahead, get an attitude about it; make it happen. Just start being nicer to people, starting right now.

You have already read examples of how people are doing this in every business niche out there. I guarantee you can do it in yours. Here is what's interesting: not only do these practices earn you massive results in business, they're actually really fun to do. It's simply an adventurous and happy way to live your life.

You will meet people and create relationships that will increase your quality of life. When you hear the word "karma," you will begin to smile instead of wince. You will be living on the positive side of the laws of attraction. What you send out is truly what comes back to you. We really believe that through kindness, we can change the world. We really believe we can bring the human race together and do it by being kind to people.

Most of us have businesses we need to run, bills we need to pay, and most of our waking hours are spent making a living. So we do relationship marketing and teach you how to be nice to people in your business because you spend most of your time there. If we can accomplish that, you're going to be nice to people everywhere. That's the key, my friends. I truly believe that with the systems we have and the philosophies we teach, you can live a life of prosperity—a life that is rich in relationships, in finance, in adventure, and in overall quality of life. By leveraging the power of human connection, you allow the abundance of the universe to flow your way.

CHAPTER 5

It's Not Who You Know that Matters

There is a popular saying that states, "It's not what you know, it's who you know that matters." Though the thought has accurate implications, it just doesn't deliver exactly what serves you. When people hear this saying they automatically think, "Well I don't know the right people, so I guess I'm out of luck."

There are two add-on thoughts that make this concept much stronger and certainly more accurate.

1. It's not who you know, it's who you get to know that matters.

2. It's not who you know, it's what you do with who you know that matters.

Now we are talking.

If you approach the concept with "who you get to know and what you do with who you get to know," then there is possibility for anyone. So how do you do those two things consistently?

I recently interviewed Jordan Adler, from Las Vegas, Nevada, a bestselling author and one of the top direct sales relationship marketing experts in the world. He also happens to be a close friend and business associate. Over the years Jordan has become a master at networking, and is a highly successful network mar-keter as well as a top producer in the sales and presentation busi-ness. When it comes to getting to know new people and doing the right things with those people, there is nobody better or more consistent than Jordan. This is precisely why he is so successful.

Everybody wants to know how top producing people become top producing people, and Jordan is just the guy to ask. Jordan credits much of his success to being a lifelong student of personal development. Back in the 90s, he read a book by Harvey Mackay, *Swim With the Sharks Without Being Eaten Alive.* One thing that struck him, and that he's always remembered about that book, is the author talking about the value of a network. The other thing he remembered about the book was the author's comment, "If you want to predict the future of someone's income, look at the size of their Rolodex."

We joked for a minute saying we had many younger listen-ers who probably don't have a clue what a Rolodex is. So for those who don't know, a Rolodex is an organized business card holder. I guess you could say it is an analog version of today's contact manager.

Jordan said he went out and bought a Rolodex and started go-ing places where people had business cards. He simply collected business cards so he could fill up his Rolodex. Then he did his best to stay in touch with those people and he looked for ways that he could add value to their lives. And he did this for years. Jordan is the king of habitual consistency, so when I heard him tell this story I could just imagine him doing this.

Early on in his career, he read another book titled *How to Sell Anything to Anyone* by Joe Girard, the top car salesman I mentioned earlier. In that book, Joe talks about networking, getting to know people, and writing "nice to meet you" notes. Jordan said Harvey Mackay and Joe Girard had a huge impact on his career, as did Tom Hopkins, author of *How to Master the Art of Selling*. So at an early age, it was anchored in Jordan's mind that building a network of people and adding value to that network was his most valuable asset.

It was in 2004 when I met Jordan for the first time. He had been introduced to my new relationship marketing system that included an online contact manager. He loved my system because it allowed him to send greeting cards through the mail from his computer. Jordan had stacks and stacks of business cards that he had collected over the years. He started putting those cards into our system and sending each of those people cards—real physical greeting cards in the mail, just to reconnect.

He would say things like, "I haven't talked to you in a while. I sure would like to get caught up. Hope you're doing great. Give me a call some time." And he put his picture and phone number in the card.

In his first week, he put 350 contacts into his new contact manager and sent out 350 cards from our system. He says that about 50 of those cards were individual cards and 300 were Happy New Year cards, where the same card went to a group list of 300 people. (Yes, our system did that even way back in 2004.)

Lo and behold, Jordan says, about four days later his phone started ringing with people that he hadn't talked to in a long time. They just wanted to reconnect. All those phone calls enabled him to springboard a new business venture with many of those contacts.

I want you to think about it for a second. How often do you receive an unexpected greeting card in the mail from an old acquaintance or friend? It's such an unusual thing and I think a lot of people underestimate the power of that. In fact, Jordan told another story, where he walked into his insurance agent's office and the first thing he noticed on his bookshelves were the six cards Jordan had sent this agent over the past couple of years. So every time that guy walks past those cards he thinks of Jordan. Now *that* is top of mind.

A tangible heartfelt greeting card that makes a connection with someone has enormous impact. People will walk into a burning building to save these tangible touches. You cannot say that about connections made in cyberspace. In fact, digital posts only last so long and then they disappear forever. You can't put a Facebook post on a shelf or have it framed so you can hang it on your wall.

If we take Jordan's story and fast forward 13 years, he has sent out about 70,000 cards and he still looks for reasons to send people cards. Today, he says 99 percent of his new business comes from referrals. The reason for that is he has accumulated 4,300 people in his contact manager over that 13 years and he sends them cards regularly. When those people are ready for Jordan's products and services, they call him. He no longer contacts anyone to initiate a business transaction.

It's not who Jordan knew when he got started. It's not even so much about who he knows today. It's what he does with who he knows that makes the difference. And because he reaches out with thoughtful cards with personalized pictures and messages to all those people, they end up introducing Jordan to new people that he gets to know. This is simple but profoundly powerful.

As you read stories like this you may get intimidated when you learn that Jordan has sent out 70,000 cards. He didn't do this overnight. In fact, he sends an average of three to 10 cards per day, and most of them are sent from his phone while he is on the run.

If you remember in Chapter 1, we talked about creating habits for mastering relationships. One of the recommended habits was to send greeting cards every day. Jordan is a level-four card sender. It's an incredibly lucrative habit he has formed. How did he send 70,000 cards? With 15 to 20 minutes of consistent card-sending every day. He has mastered the art of human connection. I guess you could say that karma is his niche.

We can also learn a tremendous lesson from Ivan Misner, also known as the "father of modern networking." He's the founder and chief visionary officer of Business Network International (BNI), the world's largest business networking organization.

Ivan started this group in 1985 and it has grown into 8,138 global chapters representing 224,000 members of BNI. Each chapter has an average of 26 to 30 members. They typically meet once a week and, let me tell you, these are not just social gatherings. In the last 12 months alone, these chapters generated 9.5 million referrals that delivered $13.8 billion in business revenue. This is an organization that gets results for people.

Ivan was a guest on my *Relationship Marketing Weekly* show recently, and he shared some amazing information about how these chapters work. There can only be one person per profession in each chapter. The core philosophy is Givers Gain®. People don't attend their weekly meetings to *get* business—they attend to *give* business. They don't ask for referrals—they give referrals. How brilliant is this? Ivan simply flipped the activity of what every networking group was doing before he came along.

"If you want to get business, you have to be willing to *give* business," Ivan says. " If you show up to *give* business, then you simply allow the reciprocation to take care of itself."

You'll remember the story he shared in the foreword to this book, about speaking to a group of 900 business professionals in London. He asked them a simple question: "How many of you are here today hoping to maybe, just possibly, sell something?" All 900 people raised their hands. He then asked a second question: "How many of you are here today hoping to maybe, just possibly, buy something?" Nobody raised their hand. Not one single person.

"This is what I call the great networking disconnect," Ivan says. "People show up to networking events wanting to sell, but they are not there to buy. "

BNI chapters are designed to change that. In his book, *Networking Like a Pro: Turning Contacts Into Connections,* Ivan says follow-up is one of the obvious keys to being a great networker. He has what he calls the 24-7-30 System. It works like this: when you meet somebody at a networking event, you want to first follow up with them **within 24 hours**. Reach out to them with a "nice to meet you" message. This could be a voice message, a text, or a greeting card in the mail. The greeting card in the old-fashioned mail is the best way to stand out, he says. And then, don't try to sell them anything.

Second, find out if they're active on Facebook or LinkedIn or Twitter, and connect with them on social media **within seven days.** By connecting, he means comment on their posts or give some feedback. Make it positive and just do it every now and then—not every day, not 10 times a day, but periodically, just make a connection. And again, don't try to sell them anything.

The third step is to reach out to them **within 30 days.** With this outreach, you can call them or you can send another card and say, "Hey, it was great meeting you a month ago. I've been following some of the things you've done online. I really found this interesting or that interesting. I would love to meet with you and learn more about what you do and if you have some time, maybe to learn about what I do." And then set up an appointment where you can sit down with them and have a one-to-one meeting. This is the beginning of the relationship-building process. Don't forget, though, whatever you do, don't sell to them even now. Give it some time. If they want your business, they will tell you.

When he was on my show, Ivan and I had a great conversation about this approach. We joked about people who think they have to be in constant sales mode. Joking, Ivan said, "I think people sometimes have sales Tourettes. They just can't stop themselves. They just blurt it out." It's natural for people who are in sales to really want to make the sale. They are looking for the home run. Often it seems they want to chase the person until they hit the home run instead of consistently creating relationships over time and allowing the home run hitter to show up naturally.

The 24-7-30 System takes patience and discipline, and a lot of people just don't have that. And it's usually because they simply don't have enough people in their pipeline. Those who are able to remain consistent with the networking approach of a pro like Jordan Adler or the subtle approach of Ivan Misner's 24-7-30 System are the ones who network with a lot of people, or with a few people consistently over time.

Those who go for the home run are the ones who feel they have to. They don't think they have enough people to prospect, so they try too hard to reel in the one they think they currently have on the hook. "This type of salesperson has a sense of desperation and the people they are talking to feel it," Ivan says. "The problem with desperation is, it's not referable."

Ivan has tremendous influence with a lot of people, and his message brings people together in business. As we were talking on the show, I asked him a question that at the time may have seemed a little off-topic. But his answer showed again the importance of relationship in how people operate in the world.

"Ivan, in our world right now we seem to have a lot of hatred. We have a lot of separation. What can we do, as a people, to bring the world back together again?" I asked.

I love his answer. He said, "I believe that I as an individual may not be able to make a world of difference. But I can make a difference in the world. I believed that 33 years ago when I started BNI. It wasn't my goal to change the world. It was my goal to change an individual life, to help one person, and then another person, and then another person. You change the world by changing individual lives. We all have people who are in our story, people who did something that changed our lives immensely. The question I like to ask is not who is in your story, but whose story are you in?"

What difference are you making in other people's lives? When you are intentional about building relationships, you put yourself in a position to make a difference. So it really is not about who you know. It's about who you get to know and what you do to be of service to them. If you follow the examples of Jordan Adler and Ivan Misner, you will consistently put yourself in a place of service to other people.

What you send out is what comes back to you. As I am writing this, I am sitting at the PB Shore Club on Pacific Beach in San Diego, California. I have noticed a homeless guy walking around here the past couple of days. He has long curly hair and a scruffy long and curly beard, and carries a sign that says he is a traveling war veteran. He has been playing a drum along the boardwalk with a money dish out in front of him. I just watched him put a dollar in the dish of another street performer. He is homeless with almost nothing to his name, and he is giving what little change he has to someone else. I'm going to take a break from writing right now because I'm going to go find that guy. I have a $20 bill in my money clip with his name on it. It looks like this dude just made karma his niche.

CHAPTER 6

Don't Ask for the Referral: Deserve It

remember the first time I said this line from the stage. It was at one of the first relationship marketing type of courses I conducted back in 2004. It just so happened that I had about 30 real estate agents in an audience of about 300 people.

When I said, "Don't ask for the referral: deserve it," I instantly felt the energy from that group shift. A few of them squirmed in their chairs, made funny faces, and started talking to each other.

If you have been to my events you will know that I am not shy when I'm on the stage. I am very interactive with the audience. I instantly stopped my speech and said, "OK, it looks like we have some folks here who are questioning what I just said. Which one of you will raise your hand and tell me what the problem is?"

A young gentleman finally raised his hand and said, "Every real estate sales course we attend expresses the importance of asking for referrals. You are now telling us not to. How can all those trainers be wrong and you be right about this?"

I answered, "Those trainers don't have a system like we have and they don't teach what we teach about relationship marketing. Because of that, they have to ask for referrals."

To illustrate this principle, I asked him to consider two scenarios. "In the first example, I send you a thank you card for attending this course today. Here's what I'll write: *Thank you for the comments you made at the event. It was a pleasure sharing a fun-filled day with you and your real estate friends. Best wishes to you and your success. Your friend Kody.* How would that make you feel?"

"Well, if you made it that personal to me I would be very impressed," he said.

"OK, here's scenario number two," I continued. "I send you a thank you card that says, *Thank you for attending this course today, we hope you enjoyed the event. We appreciate your business. If there is anyone you know who could benefit from our system or training, please don't hesitate to send them our way.* How would that make you feel?"

He paused and finally answered, "Well, when you present it like that, I see your point. Asking for the referral took away from the personalization."

"So which card would you remember most?" I asked.

"Definitely the first one," he said.

Fortunately there were other people in the room who had been using our system for a while. They had been sending thank you, birthday, holiday, and keep in touch cards consistently to prospects and customers without ever asking for a referral or anything else, for that matter. And their referral and repeat business had dramatically increased since they had been consistently doing this follow-up. A few of them took the opportunity to share their stories at this event.

Recently, I had the opportunity to interview Tom Lambert from Shadetree Automotive in Layton, Utah. Tom runs an automobile service and repair shop. "I realize that when I have someone's car all day, their whole day is disrupted and it's tough for them," he began. "It's important to be sensitive to that. When our customers pick up their vehicles, they just want to head on home and not have to think twice about their car. It's after they get home and settled that they may think of questions they should have asked, or they noticed something as they were driving the car home."

Tom sends a quick survey to his customers' phones on the day they pick up their car. It asks a few questions about satisfaction, and whether they have any concerns. They can quickly text back any questions or concerns.

Tom says there are four things he needs to do to earn people's business and their referrals:

1. Be sensitive to their inconvenience
2. Provide excellent service
3. Be informative
4. Show appreciation

The day after he sends the survey to their phones, he sends what he calls "a genuine thank you card" in the mail. He says that card usually shows up in the mail about a week down the road when they have probably started to forget about the auto repair guy.

His company's sensitivity, service, and information make a good impression, and the follow-up card keeps them top of mind. And when you are top of mind, your customers are more inclined to tell their friends, family, and neighbors about you. Tom says they have doubled their referral business over the past three years by following that system. And there is no better compliment to him than somebody trusting him enough to send another person to him.

I love stories like Tom Lambert's. He highly appreciates a referral and considers it the highest level of compliment. If more people in business had this attitude, their referrals would skyrocket. Why? Because they would take the time to incorporate best practices that generate referrals. They would not have to ask for referrals—they would deserve them.

Tom has more than doubled his referral business and has never asked for a referral. In fact, he is adamant that you don't. He says, "To say 'thank you' and then, oh by the way, 'give me' is not what relationship-building is about. They've already given me their trust to come and see me in the first place; they have given me their hard-earned money for my service. It is my turn to give, and I do that with a genuine thank you." You can't argue with Tom's attitude, his best practices, and especially his results.

IS IT EVER OK TO ASK FOR A REFERRAL?

This is a question I get all the time. My answer is YES! That may have surprised you after everything you just read.

Remember, relationship marketing is about focusing on relationships 80 percent of the time and marketing 20 percent of the time. Traditional marketing practices ask for referrals, but they typically don't do it the relationship marketing way.

WHAT IS THE RELATIONSHIP MARKETING WAY TO ASK FOR REFERRALS?

I believe it's OK to ask for referrals if you incorporate the 80/20 rule. Here is how it works.

In addition to deserving them, a great way to get referrals is to give them.

- **Give** referrals 80 percent of the time
- **Ask** for referrals 20 percent of the time.

This could be one of your marketing practices for generating new contacts for your cool market. A great activity for incorporating this is to farm your contact list.

FARM YOUR CONTACT LIST

This is a very simple activity and should be done consistently to get the best results. You simply farm your contact list and choose a minimum of five people you will reach out to every week. Your purpose is to reach out and see how you can serve them, and one of the best forms of service is to give them referrals. Don't ask these people for referrals; only give them referrals. If you do this, chances are you still won't have to ask for referrals, because people will reciprocate. But don't do this activity with any expectation of reciprocation. It doesn't work that way.

What you send out will come back to you naturally. You don't force the laws of attraction; you allow them to flow freely. What I have found is, ironically, about 20 percent of these people you give referrals to will reciprocate with referrals. There is your 20 percent, and you still have not asked.

If you do ask, I suggest you ask prospects, not customers. Here are some scenarios where you could ask for referrals:

1. When contacting your warm market to set up an appointment. If they don't have a need for your product or service, ask them if they know someone who does.

2. When you are warming up someone on your cool market list and you determine they don't need your product or service. Ask them if they know someone who does.

3. When you determine during a presentation that your prospect does not need your product or service. Ask them if they know someone who does.

Chances are, if you are farming your contact list consistently and giving out several referrals every week, you will run into people on your prospect lists you have done this for, or they might know people you have done this for. They will remember what you have done for them.

WHY SHOULD YOU NOT ASK CUSTOMERS FOR REFERRALS?

I have shifted my belief on this point. I used to teach people to ask customers for referrals only as part of a multiple-touch social media/email/card campaign. I used to say as long as 80 percent of your customer touches were about relationship only, then it was OK to ask for referrals as part of your 20 percent marketing strategy.

Here's why I have changed my position on that: the numbers don't lie. After analyzing feedback from thousands of our clients sending out hundreds of millions of follow-up greeting cards and gifts, they simply receive far more referrals from customers when they don't ask for them, versus when they do.

If you implement your relationship marketing program the right way, you should never have to ask a customer for a referral. And without question, the best referral is an unsolicited one.

SECTION 2

HOW RELATIONSHIP MARKETING WORKS WITHIN THE TRADITIONAL SALES AND MARKETING PROCESS

CHAPTER 7

Permission to Sell: The Marketing Side of Relationship Marketing

So far we have discussed in detail the power of relationships and how to network with a focus on genuine human connection. You have learned from some of the best networkers and relationship marketers on the planet.

You may be saying, "OK great, I get all this. I love it all and I want to do it. However, I don't have a network of people like a Jordan Adler. I'm brand new to the concept of BNI and other networking strategies." Or, "I just opened the doors of my new business or started a new sales position. All of these strategies you have taught, so far, take time. I need to sell some stuff now so I can put food on the table."

Don't worry—I've got you covered!

PERMISSION TO SELL

You already have permission to go sell. In fact, you have a responsibility to sell. Everyone, regardless of what they do for a living, is in sales. Make no mistake about it. Nothing in any business, or in life, happens without someone making a sale. It's what everyone does. It is also directly related to how you make connection and establish relationship with others. Selling is how the world goes around: it's how you survive, it's how you thrive, it's how we all live.

Think about it. What are the first few questions asked when you meet someone for the first time? These topics usually come up in this order:

What's your name?

What do you do? Or, what business are you in?

Tell me about your family.

What do you like to do for fun?

What you do for a living is a big part of who you are, and it's a big part of the person you are making a connection with. It's at the center of every conversation we have with others.

So if making a living is a big part of who everyone is, then why be shy about what we do and how we could be of service to others? Hopefully, you are in a line of work you are passionate about. If you are not, then you need to find your passion.

The first key to any kind of sales is to be sold yourself on what you do and what products or services you offer. If you are sold on the idea that your product or service will add immense value to the right people, then sharing your expertise is a primary way for you to add value and be of service to others.

The first time I took on a sales position I was 21 years old, and I was in between semesters in college. I had the opportunity to sell a new technology called "cellular phones" in the summer of 1985. Our flagship product was the brick phone. Remember how cool the brick phone was? It was portable—no cords or anything. It had a large battery block attached right to the phone and it worked everywhere.

I had three months before school started again and I needed to make $3,000 to satisfy my schooling budget. About four weeks into it, I got really sick and had to stay in bed for about 10 days. At the time, I was staying at my parents' house, and my room was next to the kitchen. With the door open, I could see the countertops and cabinets. I remember watching my mother opening those cabinets and pulling out food products, dishes, glasses, and utensils.

As I laid in bed watching this, I remember thinking, "If I don't get better and get out of this bed, I won't have the money to buy the food that needs to go in my cabinets at school." That was the first time I realized that selling is what makes the world go around. Somebody sold the food products, dishes, glasses, and utensils my mom was pulling out of the cabinet. Someone sold the cabinets and countertops she was working from. Someone sold the bed I was laying in. And I needed to go sell some cellular phones or I was going to be hungry. You know how it is when you're sick. Your imagination can get a little crazy when you're running a fever. I will never forget this. I think of that moment all the time.

This early experience helped me realize selling really is the key to the entire economic flow of how we live our lives. To further explain this, I've written a "Networking Sales Flow Statement," which says,

*"**Whomever you end up selling to is directly or indirectly tied to selling something themselves. Because of this, people in your network either have a need for what you offer, or they know somebody who has a need. And you either have a need for what they offer or you know someone who has a need.**"*

In the next three chapters, you will learn how to leverage this Networking Sales Flow Statement. It explains why you have a responsibility to sell things, to buy things and to provide referrals to others who sell things and buy things. This is what makes the networking sales flow work.

Let's learn from some of the best sales and marketing trainers and coaches out there, like Jordan Belfort, Grant Cardone, Tom Hopkins, Ryan Holiday, and Jeb Blount, to name a few. Obviously there are many more, and together we will share the time-tested fundamentals that will bring you massive success in sales.

One thing to keep in mind while we do this, though, is not to get too caught up in what I call "guruitis." With social media today, you see numerous posts on your newsfeed from yet another sales and marketing or network marketing guru. There is this five-step plan here and then an eight-step plan over there, and then a revolutionary three-secret formula that changes the game over there. My goodness, you can get 10 or more of these in one 10-minute scroll session on Facebook alone. Now don't take this wrong; I am all for following sales and marketing experts who have actually been top producers and offer their expertise. The problem is the myriad of people offering plans who have no real world experience to speak of.

Here is another challenge: the single most important attribute to success in sales, or anything for that matter, is consistency. So many times salespeople try one five-step plan for less than 30 days, and when they don't get immediate results, they go back to scrolling on Facebook. This is also one reason they don't get results, because several times every day they interrupt the sales-generating activities they are supposed to be doing to scroll Facebook.

And guess what they see on Facebook? You guessed it— another five-step plan that promises to be better than the one they are inconsistently trying to implement. If you can't tell, this kind of stuff drives me crazy.

At the end of the day, everything you will learn about sales has to do with three primary activities:

1. Prospecting
2. Presenting
3. Following up

The most important thing you can do is to be habitually consistent with your prospecting, presentation, and follow-up practices. The top authors and trainers mentioned in this book are experts on the modern day traditional delivery of those three things. We are going to explore those now and spice it up with our relationship marketing tactics. There is amazing information out there on this stuff. I do believe, however, that most of those traditional teachings are light in implementing relationship marketing tactics.

By the time you finish the next three chapters, you should have a good balance of traditional and relationship marketing practices. The goal is to make sure those practices are delivered throughout the prospecting, presenting, and following up process. There is a chapter on each of those disciplines; each one needs its own chapter, but keep in mind, all three are interconnected. You are prospecting through the entire process, you are presenting through the entire process, and you are certainly following up through the entire process.

Let's go to work!

CHAPTER 8

Prospect

As we begin this chapter, keep in mind it's not who you know that matters, it's what you do with who you know and who you get to know that matters. Your prospects are going to come from three primary areas:

1. Your warm market: These are people who already know, like and trust you.

2. Your cool market: These are people who know you, but you need to do some outreach to get them to like and trust you.

3. Your cold market: These are people who don't know you, so they can't like and trust you yet.

Your goal is to turn cold market into cool market, and cool market into warm market. Those who have mastered the art of selling are really good at converting cold to warm. Our relationship marketing practices dramatically enhance this process.

The first thing I would advise anyone to do, regardless of what niche you are selling in, is to make a list of everyone you know and then categorize them into a warm market and cool market list. You don't need a strong network of businesspeople to do this. There are no excuses for anyone. No matter who you are or what stage of life you are in, you can and should do this.

Use the memory jogger below to help you compile this list. You will be surprised with how many people end up on this list. The average number of people on a list like this is around 250. You may end up with many more, but get those names on a list.

Immediate family members	Your insurance agents	Who is your insurance agent
Your family relatives	Your brokers	Belongs to Chamber of Commerce
Your spouse's relatives	Who does your taxes	Who sells you clothes
Your other in-laws	Who's in the military	Who you met through friends
Who's your doctor	Works on your car	Works at your bank
Your friends	Who repairs your house	Your kids bus driver
Your parents' friends	Who cleaned your carpet	Photographs your family
Went to school with	Who delivers your paper	Friends on social media sites
Who's your dentist	Who cuts your grass	Your college friends
Who watches your children	Who sells you gas	Repairs your house
Who cuts your hair	Who waits your table	People you work with
Your kids teachers	Parents of your kids friends	People you meet in forums
Who attends church	Who reads your meter	You do volunteer work with
Your neighbors	Pest control person	People at networking meetings
Who sold you your car	You met on a plane	Who delivers your pizza
Parents of teammates	Who cuts your hair	Dry cleaned your clothes
Who you met at a party	Who sold you your home	Worked with in previous jobs
Who delivers your mail	On your holiday card list	Manages your apartment
Works at the grocery store	You meet on vacation	Manages Homeowners Assoc.
Owns a small business	Your customers/clients	Works out your gym

The next thing you want to do is get those names in an electronic contact manager of your choice. The evolution of contact lists has gone from the old school Rolodex and planner contact lists to computer-based programs like Act or Goldmine to today's SAAS (software as a service) programs that are hosted online with some kind of monthly fee. My companies have comprehensive contact management systems that are considered a SAAS at sendoutcards.com or sendogo.com. Sendogo is designed to integrate with a SAAS or CRM of your choice.

Whatever your system is, get these names in there with as much contact information as possible. Name, physical address, and email address are essential. Being able to add a phone number, birthdate, website, and social media info is ideal.

Most of today's contact managers will allow you to create groups. Make sure you have a warm market group, a cool market group, and a cold market group. Your cold market list will be created with the leads you generate from your cold market prospecting activity.

Prospecting is not just about finding people. It's about finding people and moving them from cold to warm. The warmer they are, the easier it is to close a sale. Chances are very good that right now, **you know a handful of people who would buy from you or refer a buyer to you today because they know, like, and trust you enough already. Start with those people.**

It's the standard for most to have far more people on the cool market list than on the warm market list. Again, these are people you know, but the "like and trust" part needs work. It's usually not that they don't like or trust you; it's only that you are not in contact with them enough to have the "like and trust" level where it needs to be. You want to reach out to them as well, but understand the prospecting and presentation process is different with this group. It takes more time. **Start the process with these people while you are working with your warm market people.**

Then you get to your cold market. These are people who don't know you yet. How do you reach people you don't know yet? You implement a **Cold Market Prospecting Plan.** Traditional sales professionals break this down into an inbound and outbound lead-generation effort.

Inbound includes any activity that generates a lead. A lead is someone who might be interested in your product or service. The following list of inbound activities are listed in the order of most effective to least effective:

Referrals

Website

Social media

Paid search

Sales-generated

Trade shows

Partner

Webinar

LinkedIn

Email campaign

Events

Lead list

Outbound includes any activity that reaches out to the lead that has been generated, including:

Phone calls

Text messages

Social media inbox messages

Emails

Greeting cards

These activities are all to establish rapport and schedule an appointment for a presentation.

Electronic collateral

Direct mail collateral

Greeting cards

These activities are all to provide information requested before the lead will commit to an appointment for a presentation.

Up to this point, the only thing you should be doing is setting an appointment. You should never try to sell through any of this process. The only exception to that is if someone tells you they are ready to buy now. This does happen, but don't count on paying any bills with it. We recommend you **have a daily effort that includes inbound and outbound cold market prospecting activity.**

To recap, your immediate prospecting plan should include:

1. Warm market activity
2. Cool market activity
3. Cold market activity

I'm going to give you some highly effective activities you can do in each of these areas, but before I do that, I need to emphasize how important the prospecting activity is. In his book *Prospecting*, Jeb Blount says, "The brutal fact is, the number one reason for failure in sales is an empty pipeline, and the root cause of an empty pipeline is the failure to prospect." He continues, "It's far more important that you prospect consistently than you prospect using the best techniques. Prospecting consistently means every day."

The best way to do this is to create time blocks every day for prospecting. Anything you do in the warm, cool, and cold market activities count. The key is to always keep your pipeline full of people. The more you have in your warm market, the better. Those are the ones that buy from you and refer to you. So what is a time block? It's a time you set aside every day for prospecting activity. I would suggest at least an hour a day for full-time or even part-time salespeople. It's important that when you are in a time block, you alleviate any distractions. And the number one distraction is your smartphone.

Here is the challenge: you may be using your smartphone as a tool for your prospecting activity. If you are, then you have to be disciplined to stay off social media and resist the temptation to respond to any inbound texts or phone calls during this block. Don't cheat your time block. Give your prospecting effort the attention it deserves. What you give to it will come back to you tenfold.

If you create a daily time block and stick to the warm, cool and cold activities I'm about to spell out, you will almost certainly see massive success in any kind of sales. It doesn't matter if you are selling high-tech business-to-business, real estate, insurance, car sales, motorsports, retail, network marketing, consulting service, timeshare, hair salon, medical, dentistry, chiropractic, car repair, collision repair, health and wellness—you name it, this will provide massive results for you.

You don't even have to be good at it. You just need to be consistent at it. And guess what? The more consistent you are at it, the better you will get at it. So stop complaining about your lack of success. Stop whining about what works and what doesn't. No more excuses. You don't need yet another five-step plan that will bring you success. What you do need is to be habitually consistent with your prospecting activities.

So let's jump in.

WARM MARKET PROSPECTING ACTIVITIES

People do business with those they know, like, and trust. So start some activities with your warm market list. One excellent activity is **text prospecting.** The purpose of this activity is to set appointments with people on your warm market list. This works really well with people who already know, like, and trust you.

Don't do this until you know you are ready with whatever presentation you are going to make. Please remember, you are only setting an appointment for an online/phone or face-to-face meeting. There is a reason we suggest texting. Most people are used to using the phone to set an appointment. The problem with this is that it's not immediate. Most of your phone contacts go to voicemail and it takes too much time to connect. Texting is usually immediate. You can reach a lot of people and confirm appointments at a much faster pace.

The following is a texting script that is highly effective. This is used for a phone app service that's really good for businesspeople:

Text one: *"Hey John, I would like to set up a time to show you something really cool that I think has big potential."*

The person you're texting usually will respond with something like, "Sure, what is it?"

Text two: *"It's a new technology I need to show you on your phone. When can I catch you uninterrupted for 30 minutes?"*

Now, of course you may need to slightly edit this script to fit what you are offering. But please remember to keep your message short and only have messaging to set an appointment. If your recipient tries to get you to text more, and sometimes they will, do not take the bait. Don't even begin selling them in a text—only establish the appointment.

If you happen to have a short video (less than two minutes) they could watch as an overview, you could do this:

Text: *"If I were to send you a short two-minute video, would you watch it and tell me if you are interested in learning more?"*

On occasion, I have asked my friend Jordan Adler to conduct a texting exercise using this script at our live seminars. It's really fun to watch the process. Most of the time, people in the room don't believe they can schedule appointments on the spot. Jordan takes them through the exercise where he challenges them to text 20 people in 20 minutes. Every time someone in the room confirms an appointment, he has them raise their hand and he rings a bell. I'm amazed at how many times he rings that bell within the 20 minutes. People usually set anywhere from three to 10 appointments or more within 20 minutes.

It's quick, it's easy, and it works. Keep in mind, your warm market contacts may or may not be in the market for what you have to offer, but chances are they know someone who is. If you do this correctly, you will not find that out until you go to the appointment. Remember, do not share, present, or sell in any way until you get to the appointment.

You can "text prospect" anywhere you can message someone. Texting to a phone is the obvious one, but you can also message people on Facebook, LinkedIn, or other social media platforms you use. I would not use more than one contact method per prospect. You don't want to come across like you're on the prowl. Choose the medium you feel works best for that contact and go for it.

COOL MARKET PROSPECTING ACTIVITIES

These are people who know you or know of you. Your activity with this group needs to include creating rapport or establishing relationship. **Your primary goal here is to move them from cool to warm.** That doesn't mean you shouldn't ask for an appointment. It's just a different kind of appointment. This is an appointment to reconnect, not to sell. You can use a phone,

Zoom, or live meeting to move people from cool to warm. In fact, I strongly recommend you do just that.

Through the process, they may ask you what you do and want to know more. If that happens, then set up a separate time to share your presentation. Generally speaking, you should not jump into sharing your sales presentation in this initial meeting. The reason for that is you never want them to hang up the phone wondering why you really wanted to make contact with them. Keeping these meetings separate is a great way to insure that.

It takes discipline to do this right. The best way is to create the mindset that you are truly seeking to establish relationship and not trying to make an immediate sale. You need to be genuinely interested in what they are doing and how you can establish relationship. Period.

If at some point in this process they want to know more about your product or service, you set up a separate appointment. When you finally get to where you are making your sales presentation, you should still be in the "how can I serve you" mode. After all, one of the ways for you to provide value to others is to offer your expertise. Most of the time, that includes what you are selling. Just remember that when you get someone to listen to your presentation, you are there to serve them, not to go after the hard sell. (There is more about this in Chapter 9, Presentation.)

In today's world, there are people you're getting to know online and offline. Your online circle of cool market contacts can be large and there are ways to reach them quickly.

SOCIAL MEDIA POSTS

Be active on social media. Work on your social media friend lists, and make posts for people to respond to. Make sure your posts are fun or informative. You are simply sharing your life experiences, and your wisdom and humor. This should be done on the majority of your posts. Every once in a while offer informative posts, perhaps about your chosen field of work. Don't try to sell anything, just be of service to your online friends.

As you know, I'm in the relationship marketing business. Here are some examples of some of my posts:

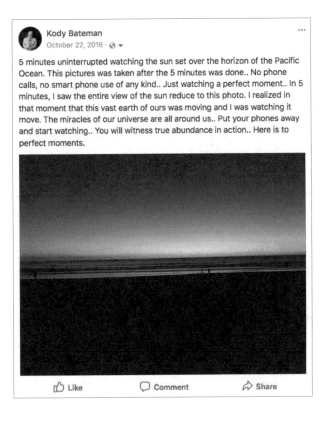

Kody Bateman
October 22, 2016 · 🌐 ▾

5 minutes uninterrupted watching the sun set over the horizon of the Pacific Ocean. This pictures was taken after the 5 minutes was done.. No phone calls, no smart phone use of any kind.. Just watching a perfect moment.. In 5 minutes, I saw the entire view of the sun reduce to this photo. I realized in that moment that this vast earth of ours was moving and I was watching it move. The miracles of our universe are all around us.. Put your phones away and start watching.. You will witness true abundance in action.. Here is to perfect moments.

👍 Like   💬 Comment   ↪ Share

Kody Bateman is with Jodi Bateman and 10 others.
December 13, 2016 · ⊙ ▾

Celebrating 30 years of adventure together.. No better place than Island Park Idaho.

👍 Like   💬 Comment   ↱ Share

Kody Bateman added 3 new photos.
February 9, 2017 · ⊙ ▾

Yup!!!

👍 Like   💬 Comment   ↱ Share

You can see the flow of my posts. The first three are simple posts sharing my life. The fourth one is a quote that lightly plays around with what I do. (My system sends out greeting cards and gifts. Our number one gift people choose is a box of brownies. Our customers always comment on how good the brownies are.) The fifth one features me at one of my events. I'm never trying to sell—just having fun and informing. I'm being of service to those who view my posts. A great book on how you can do this right is *Jab, Jab, Jab, Right Hook* by Gary Vaynerchuk.

You also want to make comments on your friend's posts—not just likes, but comments as well. Simply be engaged with your friends on social media. These activities often turn into online discussions, as you probably know. There are times when those discussions transfer to a private message, and perhaps an invitation to connect by phone or in a face-to-face meeting.

ONLINE CONNECTIONS

This includes email and making connections on social media platforms such as LinkedIn. Again, the purpose of this is to get reconnected. A natural thing to ask in these messages would be, "I would like to call you to see what you are up to." Unlike the warm market texting, you are not trying to set up an appointment to show them what you are selling; you are trying to reconnect only. If you set up a time to talk by phone, make sure that is your only intention. You are moving them from cool to warm. When you get them on the phone, use the following process under "phone calls."

OFFLINE CONNECTIONS

Phone calls

The phone is your most powerful tool. You simply need to call people. If you want to get aggressive with your cool market prospecting, you need to pick up the phone. Call people. Talk to people on this list. Get authentic about creating relationships. The purpose of calling a cool market contact is to establish re-connection. You are moving them from cool to warm.

Some of you may think, why not skip this and just text them to get an appointment? The answer is, the person on this list is probably not warm enough yet for that. You may end up booking a sales appointment on these calls, but that's not your initial intent.

Again, you want to call these people to establish a reconnection. You don't know if you are going to ask them for an appointment yet. You need to reconnect first. Make the phone call about them. How are they doing? What's new? Ask about mutual acquaintances you have. Reconnect.

....

Remember, relationship at 80 percent and

marketing at 20 percent. Always.

....

In this conversation, nine times out of 10 you will end up talking about their family, their line of work, and their hobbies, usually in that order. One of the first things you want to explore is this: see if you can send them a referral for whatever business they are in. This is the fastest way I know to move a contact from cool to warm. Even if you end up not knowing someone who needs their products or services, just the thought and attempt alone lets them know you care about them.

In this conversation, it becomes natural for you to let them know what you are doing, and in fact, chances are they will ask you. And if you have already offered a referral, they will most likely have the mindset to reciprocate.

When you are finished, send them a greeting card in the mail. Thank them for their time. Let them know how nice it was to reconnect. Don't ask for anything in the card. You are moving them from cool to warm.

If you happened to set an appointment because they wanted to see what you are doing, wait until you've had the appointment before you send the card. But always send a real greeting card in the mail after this interaction. That advice is not coming from the traditional prospecting gurus out there. It's coming from me. This is where our relationship marketing tactics will really enhance the prospecting efforts that the professional sales coaches have established; relationship marketing should be sprinkled through the entire process.

Greeting Card Connections

As you look at your cool market list, you may decide that some are better to call on the phone, while others might be better to send greeting cards to in the mail. There are several opportunities to reach out to your cool market with greeting cards.

Thinking of you cards
This card would look something like this:

You will notice the message is very short, simple, and to the
point. Notice it has a picture of the sender on the back. This is
part of the sender's personal branding and it makes you top of
mind with the person you are sending to. It also has the sender's
phone number underneath the signature. I highly recommend
including this information, to make it easy for your recipient to
contact you.

Lifestyle celebration cards

This card celebrates someone's accomplishment. Facebook
and Instagram are great places to find posts where people are
being celebrated, for anything from a new family addition to an
anniversary to a business accomplishment. While it's great to
comment on those posts, it's ten times better to send them a real
greeting card of congratulations.

You can pull these photos right from the social media post and put them on a card. Again, sign your message with your name and phone number, and have your personal branding on the card.

Birthday cards

You would be amazed at how many people do not get greeting cards on their birthday. Almost nobody receives one in the mail, especially from someone they may not have heard from in a while.

Obviously, you need to know when their birthday is and be reminded of it in time to get a card to them. Again, you can look them up on social media, download or copy their pictures, and put them on a card. You need a system that will remind you to send them a card. Sendoutcards.com and sendogo.com are the two best services available that will allow you to do everything mentioned here.

In these cards you never try to sell anything, you never ask for an appointment, you never ask for a referral, and you don't even tell them what you are doing. You only say, "Thinking of you"

or, "I'd like to reconnect!" or "Congratulations!" And if it's their birthday, you simply say "Happy Birthday!"

Your marketing is extremely subtle. It's your phone number below your signature and your picture and possibly the name of your business on the back of the card for your personal branding. That's it. A few of the cards pictured previously show this.

Let's recap the cool market prospecting process:

- Have a group list of cool market contacts.
- Focus on relationship only (getting them from cool to warm).
- Use online touches (social media, Messenger, email and LinkedIn to make contact and initiate a phone call).
- Use offline touches (greeting card connections to make contact and initiate a phone call).
- Make a phone call.
- Have a connection meeting.
- Deliver your sales presentation.

The phone call, Zoom, or live meeting you have arranged is for the purpose of establishing relationship. Find out how you can serve them. Mutual acquaintances, family, occupation, and hobbies are some general topics you can use to start the conversation. See if you can offer a referral to them. If your conversations lead to you offering a presentation of your services, then establish a separate appointment to do this.

Online connections might be more efficient in terms of time taken and the number of people you contact. However, offline connections will always be more effective in terms of making impressions and creating meaningful relationships. The best prospecting plans include the combined use of online and offline tools. The quicker you get to the phone call, the better. You can easily conclude that you need to take copious notes on your contact all the way through the process. Make sure your contact manager has a good note system, complete with reminders on what the next steps with them should be.

In the process of warming up your cool market contact, chances are they have asked you about your business and may want to know more. Because of this, setting your sales presentation appointment may come naturally.

In the event that opportunity has not surfaced, you can easily ask for it. If you have followed this process right, you have done nothing other than establishing relationship up to this point. You have been in the service of your contact. This is the 80 percent relationship part.

Never be afraid or feel guilty sprinkling in the 20 percent marketing. After all, one of everyone's biggest life quests is to make a living. Chances are you have showed interest in or even helped them with their quest already. A big way for you to continue to be of service to them is to either offer them your expertise on your product or service, or offer that to someone they care about who needs it.

As Jeb Blount says, "Be assertive. ASK ASK ASK. Ask for the appointment, ask for information, ask for the decision-maker, ask for the next step, ask for the sale, ask for what you want...When salespeople demonstrate confidence and ask assertively for what they want, prospects say yes about 70 percent of the time. Nonassertive requests have about a 30 percent success rate."

I strongly advise being assertive when the time is right, but do not rush or force this process. The relationship is the most important thing you will establish. It is far more important than any sale. Relationships last forever; a forced sale only lasts once, many times at the expense of the relationship.

If you jump into your marketing assertiveness while your contact is still cool, that definitely will not come across as cool. Make sure they are warm. Make sure they know you care about them and truly want to be of service. Make sure you have provided service to them. Make sure you have asked them lots of questions. Make sure you have been a great listener. Make sure your product or service is something they might need. Make sure you offer your knowledge to them. The warmer the contact is when you make your presentation, the less selling you will need to do. You see, they already know, like, and trust you. If they are also interested in your product, your sale is almost already made.

Many traditional sales coaches will tell you that your sales presentation is a place to establish rapport and get a contact to know, like, and trust you. Are you ready for this? I do not disagree with this idea. Ha! I probably caught you off guard with that because of how strong I am on first establishing relationship. I'm a relationship guy for sure, but I'm also a marketing guy. I believe in solid and assertive sales tactics. I believe the quicker you get to your sales presentation, the better. Just never get there at the expense of a relationship.

If you approach your presentation correctly, it can be a highly effective interaction to establish relationship. You can take a cool market contact into your sales presentation if they have asked for it or if you have invited them properly. What you have to remember, though, is they are still cool. You have to go through some extra steps to warm them up. The warmer they are going in, the fewer steps you need to take.

WHAT ABOUT COLD MARKET PROSPECTING?

You may have noticed that so far we have only talked about warm market and cool market prospecting. Traditional sales training usually talks about this process in the opposite order. They talk about cold market first and how to get a prospect from cold to warm, then to presentation and the close. Most of them do not define a cool market in between. They typically take you from cold straight to warm.

In my humble opinion, this type of training focuses far more on the marketing and sales side than it does on the relationship side. Their formula is more like 80 percent marketing and 20 percent relationship. It's all (or mostly) about the sale.

I present this in the opposite order because a relationship marketing expert will always start with their warm market. They will also have a defined list of a cool market and they will know the difference between the two. They will implement the things we have discussed so far. Their key focus will be on relationships;

getting their contacts from cool to warm and always being in the mindset of serving people. Their lists are not just contacts—they are human beings.

Any cold market prospecting should have the objective of finding new people you can put into your list of contacts, and begin the process of moving them from cold to cool. Once they are in the cool market category, you simply plug them into your cool market prospecting process.

The entire process can be visualized in a funnel. You will notice in the illustration below, there are three entry points where contacts enter your prospecting funnel. I teach you to work the bottom of your funnel first. Your warm market contacts will generate sales and referrals quickly. Their referrals plug into your cool market list where you simply work the process. I know many

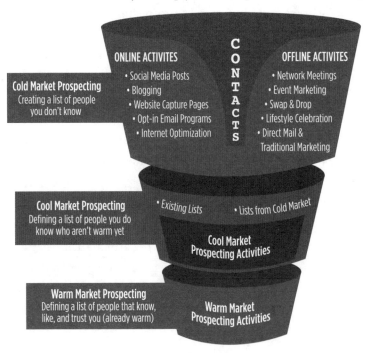

people in sales who rarely have a need to work the top of this funnel. In other words, they remain so busy from what their warm and cool markets generate, they never have to go to the cold market activities. The most aggressive plan is to work all three entry points, and both online and offline activities. The plan that will generate massive results is the one that masters the cool and warm market prospecting process.

Here is the challenge with most people in sales: they think it is easier or more attractive to sell to people they don't know. This is because they don't understand or know how to leverage the Networking Sales Flow Statement introduced in Chapter 7.

Let me fill you in on something: it's not easier to work with a cold market. I'm sure you've seen a million social media posts that claim it is. You know the ones I'm talking about:

"Never approach your family or friends again!"

"Only contact people who already want your product!"

"Plug in the leads our system provides and let our system do the selling for you!"

This all sounds attractive, but the problem is, these programs don't work for 95 percent of the salespeople who invest in them. Just remember those posts and ads are coming from people who are trying to sell you leads, systems, training modules, or live seminars. Be careful.

Now some of you are saying, "Well, Kody, aren't you also trying to sell your relationship marketing system, books, and trainings?" Yes, of course! But I know the results relationship marketing offers. My first objective is to educate people on the power of relationships. I'm detached from the outcome of selling you anything. At the end of the day, if you never buy anything from my companies, but you have learned and you implement relationship marketing in your life, I am happy.

You want to know why? Because first of all, what you are reading in this book works, and you will get massive results. It's not my theories or even statistics that prove that to be true. It's the countless stories you are reading about. If you want results, do what others are doing that generates results. This book is full of those examples.

Second, most of those sales programs that play on your fears are promising you sales results. And even if what they offer does work for you, they are generating sales for you, but not necessarily relationships. I would rather see you master relationships, because if you do, then the referral-based sales faucet generated from those relationships will never shut off.

Having said that, there are legitimate and effective cold market systems out there that can provide you with great results. Just be careful with what you believe and what you purchase. I have learned a lot about cold market prospecting, lead generation, and contact funnel systems from Russell Brunson, an online marketing genius. He is the real deal. I've learned a tremendous amount from his books *Expert Secrets* and *Dotcom Secrets*. He also offers online systems. I haven't used those personally, but if you do buy one, do your due diligence and STAY CONSISTENT with the program.

If you refer back to the funnel chart you will see the suggested online and offline activities that will generate leads or a cold market list for you. The online side mentions social media posts, blogging, website capture pages, opt-in email programs, and search engine optimization (SEO).

We already discussed social media posts as part of your cool market activities. This would also count as a cold market activity, as your online friends might share your posts or video feeds with others.

COLD MARKET PROSPECTING OFFLINE ACTIVITIES

Networking Meetings

In Chapter 5, I shared some stories from the founder of BNI, Dr. Ivan Misner. He shared his Givers Gain philosophy, where you attend your weekly chapter meeting with the intent to give referrals rather than seek them out. BNI is the largest and most effective organized networking organization in the world. With more than 8,500 chapters around the world and growing daily, BNI generates millions of referrals a year for its members. You can also meet new people in other networking organizations, such as your local Chamber of Commerce, Kiwanis clubs, and other business and social gatherings.

Event Marketing

This would include industry trade shows and various events that you could host or sponsor. Typically you would have booth or signage costs at these events. Make sure you have a solid follow-up system before you invest in a booth at a tradeshow or a sponsorship at other events. On the following page are some great examples of what you could do to sponsor, meet, and follow up with new people at events:

Swap and Drop

This is a simple concept where you swap business cards and drop a greeting card in the mail to a new person you have met. This is the perfect activity to do anywhere you meet someone new, at networking meetings and at trade shows or other events.

On the opposite page are examples of a swap and drop follow-up where a new contact was met in a public setting, at a networking event, and at a trade show.

You
Go
Girl!

Callie Shields
(713) 818-4148
callieshields@mnc.com
sendoutcards.com/freetodo

Lisa,

Wasn't the breakfast for the Women Driving Business event just amazing? I loved Carolyn Peck's advice and I definitely made wonderful high heel connections. I hope you did too. I'm excited to see you at the September luncheon. Please stop by my expo table for a chance to win a $100 in wine and goodies.

I'd love to help you drive your business – that is, making it easier to build relationships and stay in touch with clients and prospects. The fortune is in the follow up – let me show you how. Can we talk? I look forward to hearing from you.

All the best,

Callie Shields

Hi Darrell!
Great meeting you in Matteson the other day. It sounds like you have done well for yourself in Real Estate. I love talking to successful entrepreneurs about business. Hope to see you again soon!
Cheers
Jordan Adler
602 850 4440

Dear First Name,

It was really nice to meet you the other day at the event! I look forward to getting to know more about you and your business. I work with a lot of people across at different industries, and I enjoy being a connector of people if I can help in any way. I look forward to speaking to you again soon!

warmest regards,
Julie

Lifestyle Celebrations

You have already seen several examples of this in action. In fact, already in this chapter, you read about this type of card as a cool market prospecting tool. Now I'm presenting it as a cold market prospecting tool.

The story I mentioned in an earlier chapter from Gayle Zientek was a lifestyle celebration to her cold market. She did not know the guy who won the cooking contest, but by following up with a "congratulations" card, she began a relationship that has lasted for years. The story about Hugh Thompson, the State Farm Insurance guy, was a lifestyle presentation card to his cool market. The coach of the girls' basketball team knew Hugh, and this became an opportunity for Hugh to build and maintain a quality connection.

This next example took place at a boat show in Salt Lake City, Utah. I attended this event with my close friends and business associates Dave and Lori Smith. We visited the Malibu and Cobalt booth hosted by Taylor Marine. We were interested in their boats and thought they might be interested in our follow-up system. After visiting the booth, we set up an appointment to visit with them at their dealership the next week to discuss the boats we liked and to show them our follow-up system. We sent them a greeting card congratulating them on a successful boat show.

Hey Taylor,

It was great seeing you at the boat show.

Looking forward to seeing you next week.

Your Friends,

Kody B, Dave and Lori Smith

Traditional Marketing

This includes any traditional advertising or marketing efforts, such as radio, television, newspaper or magazine advertising and numerous forms of direct mail. As an example, people in real estate are taught to "farm local neighborhoods," where they choose a neighborhood and send a mail piece or place door hangers throughout the chosen neighborhood. The following is an example of a greeting card being used to farm a local neighborhood. This is an example of a direct-mail piece used to generate leads for their cold market list.

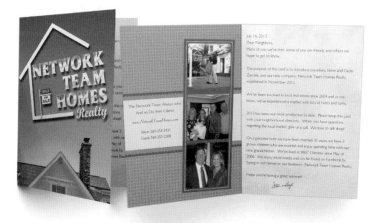

All of these activities are designed to meet people and move them from cold to cool to warm, and then on to presentation, to close, and to the ongoing relationship that generates referrals. The goal through all of this is to get them to a presentation of your offering. Let's move on and explore the dynamics of a relationship marketing style presentation.

CHAPTER 9

Present

Now it's time to present your product or service. This is where the rubber meets the road in your marketing and sales process. As I already mentioned, I'm going to give you the relationship marketing version of how to present your offering.

Rule number 1: When you get someone to listen to your presentation, you are there to serve that person, not to go after the hard sell. In your presentation, the more they talk the better. You want them to talk about their own pain, the pain your product or service has a solution for. And you want them to say the word "yes" to questions that validate the use of your product or service as much as possible.

How do you do this? You ask the right questions and listen closely to their answers. Unfortunately, most salespeople don't do this. They typically go into their feature pitch and explain everything their product and service can do. I will give you an example of this with the products and services that I offer.

I'm in the relationship marketing business. I offer products and services that help business people stay top of mind with their prospects and customers. We offer turnkey follow-up systems that deliver personalized tangible touches in the mail. We primarily deliver those touches with real greeting cards and gifts. We bridge the gap between high-tech and personal touch with modern technology.

With your smartphone, you can take a photo of a prospect or customer, load it onto a greeting card, type or voice into your phone the personal message you want to share, put your own branding on the back of the card, and click send. Our system will print the real greeting card, stuff it into an envelope with a first-class stamp, and send it for you in the mail. You can even add a gift to that card and pre-schedule campaigns to go out automatically. The system includes a contact manager that will store your contacts, remind you of upcoming birthdays and other occasions, and make it convenient and fast to follow up with your customers and help them feel appreciated. If you have your own CRM or contact manager, I have a separate company that will integrate your system with ours so you can apply our system from the convenience of your own.

So there you go. That's what I do. That is what I offer. Now some of you might be thinking right now that I wrote this to pitch you on my products and services. Some of you are probably saying, "There it is, Kody finally pitched us and he wants us to buy something more than just this book." The reason that some of you might be thinking this is because even though what you just read is informative, it sounds like a pitch. It sounds like something you would read in a product brochure. It is feature-rich, not benefit-rich.

This means I'm highlighting all the things my system can do. I'm not highlighting yet what it has done for the businesspeople who have used it. Also, novice salespeople typically learn the feature pitch and they verbally "throw up" on their prospects with it. We should all know features don't sell; benefits do. But that's not even the worst of it. By unloading the feature pitch, you make the presentation all about you. By doing this, you lose the caring connection you have, hopefully, worked so hard to build.

I wrote this only to explain what my business offering is. I want you to know that so you will understand what I'm about to share with you. I'm about to share how to present this information by asking and answering questions in my presentation. By doing this, I am continuing to build rapport and trust with you through the process. I am always in the mindset of moving you further into the warm category. Even in the presentation. I don't want to come across like I'm trying to sell you. I want to come across like I truly want to help you, because that is truly the goal when you're building relationships. Now you know what not to present and you know the elements that are needed for how you should present.

Here's how this works in action. I was recently in the office of a friend that I buy off-road vehicles from. His name is Paul Weller, of Weller Recreation in Kamas, Utah. My company had just developed a new service that I knew his dealership needed. I was meeting with him to discuss the possibilities.

I started asking Paul questions about his business. It started out simple. "How is business?" I asked. He had recently moved into a new and much larger facility, so he talked about the move and how he needed to manage a larger inventory of products.

This triggered my next question: "Does your new facility attract enough sales to offset increased overhead?" He laughed and answered, "That's what we ask ourselves every day around here." He said the new facility did generate more sales, but it was a bit more challenging to manage it all.

This triggered the next few questions: "How do you project sales when you go to order products from your manufacturers?" and, "What kind of CRM system do you use, and do you like it?"

These questions generated a discussion about the upside and downside of his business. Once he sensed that I was genuinely interested, he couldn't stop talking about his pain. His CRM did not allow him to do some of the things he needed to manage his customers. He figured he could generate more sales if he had better ways to follow up with his walk-in traffic. He also wanted to reach out more to his existing customers. He said his system triggered some decent email and social media touches, but he thought they could make improvements.

Being one of his loyal customers over the years, I had always reached out to and dealt with one of the three Weller brothers who own the dealership. I knew those three guys genuinely cared about me and their other customers.

So, I asked him, "With your expansion of sales reps and parts and service people, how do you create the same level of caring service that you and your brothers offer?"

"That's exactly what our issue is," he answered. "We want our customers to know, like, and trust the other people that work here so we need ways to do that."

This triggered my next line of questions:

Question: You mentioned that your CRM triggers email and social media touches to your customers. What other kind of follow-up communication do you do?

Answer: We don't.

Question: You mentioned foot traffic in your showroom. How do your salespeople follow up with those potential buyers?

Answer: They usually don't unless they get a phone number. If they do, it's usually a text or phone call.

Question: I know that you and your brothers get referral business all the time. How often do your other sales reps get referral business?

Answer: They don't.

Question: I gather you would like your new sales reps to generate more sales from walk-in business?

Answer: Of course.

Question: I'm sure you would like to see them generate their own referral base of business.

Answer: Yes.

Question: You want them to convey the same level of caring service that Weller's is known for?

Answer: Yes.

Paul knew I had a relationship marketing fulfillment service. In fact, he and his company had used our service in the past. The reason they did not keep using it is because they needed it to work within their CRM. With that in mind, the questions continued.

Question: Do you and your reps enter new prospects and customers into your CRM?

Answer: Either they do or our finance people do when a sale has been made.

Question: If you could trigger our follow-up card and gift campaigns within your CRM would you see that as a solution to your issues?

Answer: So you are saying I can trigger your service in my CRM?

Notice what just happened. Paul is now starting to answer my questions with questions. This is when you know someone is really interested in what you are offering.

I answered, "Yes. We have been working on an integration service that triggers our card and gift campaigns to work within your system."

"How do we get started?" he asked.

What I did was engage Paul with a carefully scripted list of questions that got him to talk about his pain. What I did not do was immediately start pitching him on my solution. I just kept asking him questions. Four of his answers acknowledged the pain he was feeling. The next four answers involved Paul saying yes to the solution I was offering. His final comment was him literally asking for the order. I didn't discuss features at all. Those are things he and his team can learn after the order has been placed.

Let me pause here to explain something that's very important. I used this approach because I was genuinely intrigued with his business and really did want to know how I could help him. And, you know what? Paul felt that. Does it always run this smoothly? No, but the warmer they are when you start this process, the more likely it will run this smoothly.

In the case of this story, Paul already knew about my company and my offering. Because of that, the questions or the **what I ask** part of my script was enough to close the deal. Most of the time, I also need to use the presentation or the **what I say** AND **what I do** part of my script to close the deal. You'll notice I used the word "script." This word scares many people. It scared me for years. I didn't like scripts. I thought they took away from the authenticity of my sales presentations. I was wrong.

What I have learned over the years is that you cultivate authenticity when you carefully listen to people and respond to their pain. The feeling of authenticity is generated from what you hear, not from what you say. If I am thinking about what I'm going to say next in a presentation, chances are I don't fully hear what my prospect is saying.

If you fully script what you need to ask, say, and do, then you don't have to be consciously thinking about what you need to ask, say, and do. This gives you the freedom to stay conscious with what you need to hear. This is how you always keep the presentation about them instead of about you.

A good script will always include things you need to **ask**, things you need to **say**, and things you need to **do**. You want to be unconsciously competent with what you ask, say, and do, so you can stay conscious with what you hear.

Right this second you might be saying, "Wait a minute, did I just read that twice?" Yes you did, and if my editor would have allowed it, I would have written it maybe three more times. Why? Because repetition is how you move from conscious to unconscious. Be unconscious with what you ask, say, and do so you can stay conscious with what you hear. That is what a good script will do for you. This is the key to mastering relationship marketing style presentations. The better you get at it, the more you can focus on the needs of those you are presenting to.

If you are still not convinced that detailed scripts are essential to your presentation, consider this explanation offered by Jordan Belfort in his book *Way of the Wolf*: "Since the time that you were old enough to talk, every single movie or TV show that made you laugh or cry or scream or shout, or that got you so deeply invested in the characters that you ended up binge-watching the entire series in a single weekend; every last one of them was scripted. So if you want to hang on to the false belief that using a script is going to make you sound wooden and inauthentic, because sounding wooden and inauthentic is an inherent characteristic of using a script, then you need to ignore the fact that you have spent about half of your life being made to laugh and cry and scream and shout as a result of—yes, you got it: scripts."

RELATIONSHIP MARKETING SALES SCRIPT FORMAT

I'm not going to write your script for you. That would not be possible because I don't know your business or offering the way you do. What I do know is you can follow a script format to formulate your own. And it works for any type of business you are in. It's as simple as this:

What I ask

1. Ask questions that get your prospect to feel the pain that your offering has a solution for.

2. Ask questions that get your prospect to say "yes" to things they need that you can offer.

3. Ask questions that get your prospect to say they need and want to order what you offer.

What I say

1. Say things in your presentation that highlight their pain and offer solutions to their pain.

2. Say things in your presentation that highlight you having an offering to what they have said "yes" to.

3. Ask for the order.

What I do

1. Discuss benefits: features tell, benefits sell. A feature is what your product or service does; a benefit is what your product or service delivers.

Feature: Our relationship marketing system reminds you of birthdays and special occasions.

Benefit: Simply by sending out birthday cards, we received a 50 percent increase in referral business in the last 12 months.

2. Tell stories that feature testimonials. The best way to present benefits is in a story. People love stories.

3. Be prepared for objections. Prepare a list of all the objections you have ever heard or you can think of about your product or service. Know what they are and be prepared when you are faced with them. A great solution to objections is the "feel, felt, found" approach. This is where you say, "I can relate with how you feel. I felt the same way when I first heard about this. This is what I found." And then you finish that with an answer to the objection.

4. Ask for the order. Surprisingly, most salespeople make the mistake of not asking for the order. A number of studies conclude the optimum number of times a salesperson should ask for the order is somewhere between five and seven times. I believe if you master our relationship marketing version of prospect, present, and follow up, you will only need to ask for the order a few times. But you still need to ask for the order. This format will help you to dial in on exactly what you should have in your script.

Let me show you an example of this in action. Again, keep in mind I am in the relationship marketing business. I'm going to share how I have incorporated this to prepare a script for our sales presentations.

In using this script format, I started out with a challenge. It seemed difficult to highlight the pain someone felt by not having my product. Think about it: what is the pain in not sending greeting cards and gifts? There are other products and services where it's much easier to recognize the pain.

People feel the pain of being overweight, so they buy weight loss products. People feel the pain of no energy, so they buy coffee or an energy drink. People feel the pain of an unreliable vehicle, so they buy a new car. The list goes on and on:

Flabby muscles: gym membership
Fear of accidents, death, sickness: insurance policies
Need for affordable home: real estate agent
Properly fitted clothing: apparel store
Need for better income opportunities: education
Increase sales: sales education, sales tools
Keep track of business needs: computer, CRM service, management tools

My companies offer fulfillment of tangible touches featuring greeting cards and gifts. A mistake we made for years was branding ourselves as a greeting card and gift company, not as a relationship marketing system. We have since made that shift, but many of our sales reps continue to present us as a greeting card and gift solution.

Here is the challenge: how do you highlight the pain of not sending greeting cards and gifts? Individuals and companies, in their minds, don't need to send cards and gifts. In other words, they don't obviously see or feel the pain of not doing so. We needed to create a script that highlighted the pain and featured the increased sales, better retention, and relationship building benefits of using our service.

We always start by having people sample our service. We load our app onto their smartphone and have them send a card from their phone to someone who is close to them. We do this because this experience has an emotional impact on the person sending their first card. We also do this because they immediately see the value this tool could have in their personal and business life. We usually don't need to tell them this when they experience it for themselves.

After they have experienced our service we go into the scripting:

What I ask

How do you feel when you buy a product or service and you don't feel appreciated?

Does it affect the relationship you have with that person or company?

Do you wonder why they don't reach out more to you?

Are you prone to complain or desire to move your business?

How often do you feel underappreciated in your personal relationships?

Here is the kicker: if someone asked those questions about you, what would your customers or friends say? Now they are feeling the pain, but just to make sure the pain kicks in, we further highlight the pain.

What I say

How you make your customers feel is more important today than ever before. You want to know why? Because the Google and social media world has changed everything. People know about you, your product, and your service before you interact. They also comment on social media about you. And, they are 11 times more likely to post a negative experience than they are a positive one. Because of this, relationships today will make or break your business faster than anything. Then I go back to asking questions.

What I ask

With this in mind, do you see the value of making sure your prospects and customers feel appreciated?

If you had a system that was more effective than email and social media to stay top of mind with your customers, would you use it?

Would you benefit from more referral business?

If our system helped you increase sales, retain more customers, and strengthen relationships, would you purchase it?

Then, if needed, we use customized questions that pertain to the prospect's specific business.

You can see examples of this in the type of questions I asked Paul Weller in the story I just shared. If he didn't already know about our product and service, I would have used this scripting from the beginning to the end. But Paul was already sold on what I offered. He needed to learn the benefits of how we could integrate with his CRM. So I simply fast-forwarded to the customized questions that pertained to his dealership. He asked me for the order, so I did not need to continue with what you see below.

What I do

At this point, we share success stories of others using our service, including results they have received. We go into examples of how the product works. We go over options and pricing, and we ask for the order.

You don't need to use this script format in its exact order. Sometimes you don't even need to use certain parts of it. I showed you an example of that with the Paul Weller story.

The way you use your script will vary based on three things:

1. How warm your prospect is at the time of your presentation.

2. How they respond to your questions.

3. How much you know about their specific needs.

If you have a well-written script created with this format, you want to study and memorize it. Know your script inside and out. If you do, you can focus on listening and you can tailor your presentation to their needs with word-for-word scripted responses that get results.

Many sales organizations offer variations of this scripting within a carefully crafted presentation package. With today's technology, it's usually built in some kind of electronic sales deck (that's a fancy sales term for a Keynote or PowerPoint type of presentation tool). Sometimes, there is video embedded in these presentations. If these are done correctly, they are super cool. They are professional, colorful, and full of all the right selling points. They usually follow a specific script.

CHAPTER 10

Follow Up

We have been discussing the importance of follow-up throughout the networking and prospecting process. It's obvious how important it is after the presentation. We have already learned from Ivan Misner that follow-up is one of the keys to becoming a master at networking and he gave us one really cool strategy called the 24-7-30 Systems.

Now we are going to discuss follow-up as one of the keys to making money. And I'm going to share some interesting statistics, and strategies. This information will help you become a master at follow-up.

If the fortune is in the follow-up, then what is the best way to follow up? Everyone seems to know the fortune is in the follow-up, yet few people have a follow-up plan or system. In fact, 48 percent of salespeople **never** follow up and 90 percent of salespeople make fewer than three contacts. And here's the kicker: 80 percent of sales and referrals are made between the fifth and twelfth contact.

That means if you simply reach out to your prospects and customers more than five times, you will be in the top twentieth percentile of sales generation. Here are examples of what counts as a contact.

Digital:

- text
- inbox (email or personal message)
- social media
- phone call

Tangible:

- direct-mail collateral
- greeting cards
- greeting card/ gift combination
- meeting in person

WHAT ARE THE MOST IMPACTFUL TYPES OF CONTACTS?

Without even sharing statistics, you can put yourself in the shoes of the receiver and tell me which type of contact is most impactful. When we ask this question at our relationship marketing events around the world, we ask people to put themselves into two categories:

1. Prospect: someone is seeking to acquire you as a customer.
2. Customer: someone you do business with is staying in touch.

Under each of these scenarios, you have already been contacted by someone and they are following up with you or simply staying in touch. Think of a specific item you had interest in or purchased, such as a home, car, insurance, etc. What kind of contact has the most positive impact on you?

The top three answers vary depending on what you are buying and where you are in the decision-making process. However, they typically include these types of contacts:

Prospect
1. Text or inbox with personalized message and link to provide more information
2. Greeting card thank you
3. Phone call

Customer
1. Greeting card and gift thank you
2. Social media recognition
3. Phone call or text

This exercise shows that a thank you greeting card shows up as a top three impactful contact for both a prospect and a customer. To be more specific, it's a thank you greeting card for a prospect and a thank you greeting card with a gift for a new customer. What's interesting is that many studies indicated that as high as 97 percent of salespeople never send a thank you card to a customer, and almost nobody sends a thank you card to a prospect. This leads me to believe that if you simply mastered the activity of thank you cards, you would be part of the 3 percent using the most impactful follow-up contact. This is the single most important impression you can make on a prospect, a customer, or someone in your personal life. I realize you have read this over and over again in this book, but it can't be said enough.

So far, I have only discussed the initial follow-up contact. There have been numerous sales studies done by sales professionals showing that the majority of sales and referrals happen between the fifth to twelfth touch. That means you need to contact your prospect or customer anywhere from five to 12 times before any business transaction takes place. But I want to show you something interesting. Those studies typically give you examples of how those prospects or customers are being reached:

· Automated email (usually triggered by a CRM)
· Direct mail (surveys, collateral, postcards from a CRM)
· Social media (Facebook, Twitter, LinkedIn, Alignable)
· Phone calls (leaving voice messages)
· Face-to-face meetings
· Greeting cards
· Greeting cards with gifts

These touches are typically used in this order. The further down this list you go, the less likely that type of touch is used. What this means is that sales or referrals are generated between the fifth and twelfth touch, where the majority of those touches are the top four on this list.

So why do most people predominantly use the top four? Simple. There is usually some kind of system that automates those touches for them. If they don't have a system, they usually don't follow up at all.

We have already established that the most effective touch by far is an immediate follow-up thank you card to a prospect and a follow-up thank you card with a gift to a new customer. You make these even more effective when you:

1. Send them out immediately.
2. Make them personal with pictures or messages.
3. Only say thank you.

Just imagine, if you will, that your follow-up touches always included this type of initial thank you. How much more effective would your follow-up system be? Would it still take between five to 12 touches before any transaction took place? I haven't done that study and I can't find one that has been done. Someday I will have this study conducted just for fun even though I don't need to—I already know the result.

Again, put yourself on the receiving end of these touches. How much more quickly will you do business or give referrals to someone who starts their follow-up campaigns in this manner? I already shared with you my personal story of shopping for the Ford truck. If I had received a prospect thank you card with my picture next to the truck I'm interested in with a simple thank you message, there's absolutely no question I would be driving that new truck right now. I also would have referred three of my friends who were interested in the same truck.

I would love to do a study of several salespeople from any industry. For fun, let's just stick with the auto sales industry. This would be a side-by-side study that compared a group of salespeople. The first group only does single touch follow-ups, a thank you card to a prospect, and a thank you card with a gift to the new buyer. The second group does the standard five- to 12-touch follow-up campaign using an automated system, which sends the auto-email, the direct-mail pieces, and social media touches; they also manually send texts and perhaps make phone calls.

After 12 months of consistent activity, which of these two groups do you think would generate the most sales and referral business? We can't know the answer for sure before that study is done. But I would bet your hypothesis is the same as mine: we believe the first group that sent the tangible touch follow-up would win.

I've already mentioned the only thing better than a thank you card is multiple cards and other forms of touches throughout the year. So another study might look like this:

The first group—In addition to the prospect thank you card and new buyer card with gift, they add a birthday card and a holiday card. They also include email, social media, text, and phone call touches.

The second group—Just like the first group, they do the standard five- to 12-touch follow-up campaign using an automated system. That system sends the auto-email, the direct-mail pieces, social media touches, manually send texts, and perhaps add phone calls. So now, which group wins and by how far?

Recently, I interviewed Chris Kendall on my *Relationship Marketing Weekly* show. He is a second-generation 20-year car sales veteran based in Louisville, Kentucky. He has a rule that he lives by: after selling a car, before the taillights leave his lot, he sends his customer a thank you card with a box of brownies. The card has a picture of the car buyer next to the car they just purchased, a short but personal thank you message, and his picture on the back of the card.

Congratulations Renee!

Dear Renee,

I wanted to send this out to say thanks again for doing business with me.

Please feel free to call me or stop by anytime I can be of assistance.

Ps. Enjoy the brownies!
I added a few more for the office staff.
Please tell everyone happy New Years for me.

Your friend & New favorite car salesman:)

Chris

He also captures his customer's birthday at the time of purchase. With our system, he builds a birthday card and adds a picture of the customer's car along with a quick happy birthday message. Again, he puts his own picture on the back of the card, saves it in our system, and the system automatically sends that birthday card seven days before the customer's birthday.

This will look good in your driveway Shonessi!

WISHING YOU ALL THE BEST
ON YOUR SPECIAL DAY!

Dear Shonessi,
I wanted to send this out to say thanks again for thinking of me, it really meant a lot!
Hope you have a great Birthday Shonessi!
Your favorite car salesman:)
Chris.   Ps. enjoy the brownies!

He also has the system automatically send a Christmas card to that buyer.

Dear Owens family,

I want to take this opportunity to let you know how much I appreciate you and thank you for the role you play in my life.

Merry Christmas to you and your family & wishing you all a healthy, happy & prosperous 2018.

Your favorite card sending car salesman,

Chris

Here is what's interesting. Chris started using our system early in November. He started implementing everything you just read. Part of that activity included creating a group list of previous buyers that he sent a Christmas card out to, and birthday cards to those whose birthdays he had captured. He said after 20 years of selling cars, he had his single biggest car sales month in January, only two months after starting this practice. And January is typically the slowest sales month of the year.

I want to reference again our company's method of implementing a relationship marketing program (see the chart on the opposite page). Most of this is done within the follow-up campaign activity. Notice we have the thank you, birthday, and holiday as the hub of the activity. We recommend those touches to be tangible, personalized, and sent with appreciation only—without asking for anything. The example we just gave of Chris Kendall utilizes only the thank you, birthday, and holiday. He currently doesn't use any of the other touch suggestions, and yet he is getting phenomenal results.

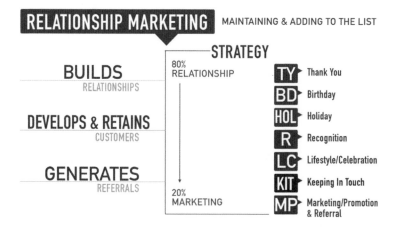

This chart will remind you of all the possibilities you have to build the perfect follow-up campaign for your own business. As a reminder, lifestyle celebration touches, though they may take a little more effort, have an enormous effect. The keep in touch and marketing touches can be with greeting cards or more of the standard methods such as email, social media inbox, texting, phone calls and face-to-face meetings.

Remember, people like to be appreciated, but they also like to be informed. If your specialty is car sales, real estate, insurance, car repair, business-to-business sales, or something similar, then follow up as the professional informant to your prospect. Again, the more you're informing and not selling, the better.

The better you get at follow-up, the more your contacts will reach out to you themselves or send a referral to you when they are ready to buy. You really don't need to be the pitcher. You can be the catcher.

In some of my live events, I tell a story about my dogs, Gus and Ruger. Both dogs love to fetch tennis balls. But they do it differently.

Gus gets so excited to fetch the ball that he takes off running before I even release the ball. The ball will land out in front of him and he will chase it until he can grab it in his mouth. When Gus returns with the ball he does not want to let it go.

Ruger, on the other hand, keeps his eye on the ball. He waits until I throw the ball and he gets underneath it and catches it in midair. When he returns the ball, he immediately releases it. He is ready to go again.

There are many metaphors in this story. The sales metaphor is that Gus sees the ball as a sale. Ruger sees the ball as a person. Gus is on the chase; he takes his focus off the person and chases the sale. When he catches it, he mauls it to death and doesn't want to let it go. In other words, he keeps selling; he is focused on what he can get from the catch.

Ruger keeps his focus on the person. He has fun, creates a connection, keeps eye contact and nourishes the relationship. He simply waits for the sale to come to him. When it gets there, he doesn't have to chase it, he catches it. When he brings it in he releases it. In other words, he stops selling and begins nourishing relationship again. He just wants the ball back up in the air so he can have fun with his new friend. He is focused on what he can give to the person. He doesn't see it as a sale at all.

Let's relate this to my story about looking at the new Ford truck. The sales guy viewed me as a sale. He was only interested in chasing the sale. The only time he followed up with me was to try to sell me at a higher price than I was willing to pay.

Even when his year-end offers made his pitch more attractive, he continued to chase the sale. His two methods of communication were text and voicemail. In each, he only talked generalities about the deal itself. He never asked how I was doing, and he didn't even say the words "thank you" at any time. Not once. He was chasing the sale. He mauled me to death and, frankly, ticked me off. That's like Gus chasing the ball and mauling it to death.

If he would have sent the thank you card after the initial meeting, and then again after the next interaction via text and voicemail, he would have made the sale. That is like Ruger keeping his eye on the ball and having fun with it. If the ball is a person and not a sale, you can get up under it and wait for the sale to come to you.

If your follow up is to a potential sale and that is your mindset, you will get moderate results with low referral business. If your follow up is to a person and that is your mindset, you will get massive results with high referral business.

I want to go back to the story of Chris Kendall. When he was on my show he talked about his father. Chris is a second-generation car salesman and he learned a lot from his dad. He shared with us that when his father passed away, more than 100 people at his wake were customers who had purchased cars from him over the years. I was so impressed with this. What kind of salesperson do you need to be to get your customers to attend your wake?

Chris told us a heartfelt story about his dad that transformed his sales career. Chris went to his dad's home one evening. His dad, who was getting on in years, was working with large stacks of paper files. Chris asked what he was doing. His dad said, "These files are of all my customers that I have worked with over the years. I want to make sure these people are taken care of." His dad was putting the customers' files into piles and assigning each pile to a salesperson he thought would best match the personality of the people in those files.

Chris was emotional as he told us how impressed he was with this. Here was his dad, no longer actively working, but wanting to make sure his customers were taken care of. There was no monetary gain for his father in doing this. To his dad, Chris said, those files represented people: they were not prospects or customers—they were friends. Chris's father was still following up with his customers even after he wasn't selling cars anymore. He is still following up with those people through others today. This, my friends, is the power of human connection. This is what genuine follow-up is all about.

CHAPTER 11

Taking Care of the Home Team

R egardless of their position, everyone has a home team. A business owner has employees who make up the home team. An independent or inside sales representative has a home team. Engineers, ITS developers, marketing specialists, franchisee owners, dealerships, professional and healthcare specialists—you name it. Everyone has home teams.

These are the people who back us up—those who take care of all the details. Whether they are in customer support, accounting, marketing, legal, production, fulfillment, facilities, or other critical functions, it's the home team that makes things happen.

Often when we are in senior management, ownership, or sales positions, we get the idea that what we do matters most. After all, if a company doesn't sell something then there is no revenue to take care of the home team, right? As an executive who has been in sales or ownership positions for the majority of my career, I must confess I had this mindset. The home team was my support. They were there to back me up and do what I needed them to do. They got paid to do what I told them to do. I have learned that even though this seems like a logical process for how business is conducted, it is sheer stupidity to think this way.

I have learned that, as an owner or a sales executive, I am simply a member of the home team. I am no more important than any other member of that team.

I've noticed this mindset creates a big challenge in the direct sales, network marketing, dealership, and franchise sales arenas. In these environments, the outside sales channels have often invested money and are driven by residual commissions and they thrive on praise and recognition. Because of that, they sometimes get carried away with their own self-promotion and importance.

I applaud these business models and have made millions of dollars being part of them. I also have a network of thousands of others who have created business success in these models. I think it is a fantastic model—right up until I see some of those people downplay and mistreat members of the home team who back them up. They start thinking they are somehow more important. I have news for them: they are not more important. Nobody is more important than anyone else.

I have actually heard independent sales reps state from generic sales training stages, "The home team at corporate is there only to pay commissions and get the product out on time. Other than that, they should stay out of our way."

Are you kidding me? The home team is just that—a team. They are your team. You are simply a member of that team. As an owner or senior sales executive you might be considered the quarterback or the coach. Because of that you get recognized more and paid more. But a quarterback who doesn't appreciate or realize he is only as good as the front line protecting him will not last long as the quarterback.

Taking care of the home team is one of the most important things a business can do. It starts with excellent training and internal communications. It requires everyone to understand the mission of the company, not only what you do and how you do it, but also why you do it.

The mission at my company is very clear. We are out to help millions of people to act on their promptings to reach out in kindness every day. We are out to change the world, to create a kinder society in business and in personal life. Those who work at my company know this and they buy into it. They believe in the mission and they put their hearts and souls into it.

As the owner I would like to take credit for that, but I really can't. First of all, we hire amazing people. They show up with good hearts, sound minds, and amazing talents. We simply teach the mission and the fundamentals of incorporating that mission and we allow our team to govern itself. For example, we give our customer support representatives full authority to do whatever they need to do to make our customers happy. They don't have to get supervisor approval. They simply do what they feel is best. We believe in them and we want our customers taken care of quickly.

Does this ever come back to bite us? Sure it does, but that is the exception, not the rule. What you send out comes back to you. We send out our confidence and trust to our team members who take care of our customers. Because of this, they are motivated to be a solution to our customers' needs. They go out of their way to make things right for people. As a result, our customers feel appreciated.

Over the past several years, I have received hundreds of greeting cards in the mail from customers telling me how much they appreciated a specific customer support person who took care of them. They want to make sure a member of our home team is properly recognized. I am also blessed to have an incredible management team. From onboarding new employees, to training, recognition, and the creation of a winning team culture, the leaders on my team are the best at it. Again, I teach the mission and then do my best to stay out of the way. I have a weekly meeting with my senior team to make sure the mission and the daily operations stay balanced. When you send out trust, you get back trustworthy people.

There is a simple three-step formula that works wonders for taking care of the home team.

1. Trust
2. Educate
3. Appreciate

If you consistently do those three things, your home team will perform miracles for your business every day. They will also enjoy their job more and that means better retention and more efficient and competent operations.

My dear friend Gregg Bryars is a master at appreciating his home team. Gregg is a senior vice president over operations for a national healthcare company. They have more than 4,000 employees and Gregg oversees 1,200 members of this massive home team.

When he visits his offices, Gregg does what he calls a walk-about, where he walks the building and talks to employees. On one of these walkabouts, he ran into a janitor named Derek Brown. He learned that Derek is from Jamaica. He came to America with his son who competes as a long-distance runner.

As Derek told his life story to Gregg, a human connection was made. Gregg pulled out his smartphone, took a picture of Derek and sent him this card:

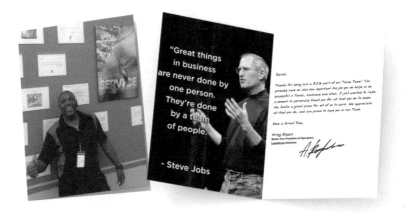

When the big boss walks through the facility, takes the time to stop and make a connection such as this, and then captivates the moment by sending a real card with pictures and kind words, do you think that makes a difference? This card is an example of what Gregg calls a "caught in the action" card. He has sent 40 to 50 of these cards to random home team members over the past several years. He also sends personal employment anniversary cards and birthday cards to his entire staff, and sends a Christmas card to his management team with a gift every year. I have learned so much from Gregg Bryars. He makes friends with people everywhere he goes. He is always conscious about people around him and he goes out of his way to make connections.

Gregg is also a tenacious businessman. He is really into numbers and statistics and return on investment. When he started in this VP position, his departments experienced an annual turnover rate of 70 percent. So out of 1,200 employees, they would turn over approximately 840 people a year. By the time they exited out an employee, replaced them, and then onboarded someone new, they figured their average cost of doing so was around $10,000 per employee. That is approximately $8,400,000 per year in expenses. Wow! Dollar amounts add up quickly when you are dealing with that many people.

Within a year of implementing what he calls his employee retention plan, he had increased retention by 30 percent. So instead of turning 840 people, they were now turning only 480. That is 360 fewer turnovers per year times $10,000, or approximately $3,600,000 in savings.

What was his employee retention plan? Simple:

1. Trust
2. Educate
3. Appreciate

His appreciation initiatives, which were cards and gifts, cost him around $7,500 per year, for a $3,600,000 return. After doing this for a few years, his company CEO caught wind of it and began sending employee anniversary cards. He now sends those to more than 4,000 employees every year.

Another powerful example comes from Dean Gialamas who works with a law enforcement agency that employs 18,000 people. I recently had the opportunity to interview Dean and this is what he shared in his own words:

> I work for a law enforcement agency that has 18,000 employees. I have 1,300 people in my command or area. I actually find a tremendous value in using the power of the written word in a heartfelt card with gifts that just create

amazing relationships with our employees. When you look at business budgets, most of their budgets are spent on employees. So you want to keep your employees happy. You want to keep them engaged. You want to keep them excited about being there. What's amazing is that with the power of the written word, I can go into offices of employees and they still have the card I sent them four or five years ago sitting on their desk. And when I ask them, "Why do you still have that?" they say things like, "No one has ever done this before. No one appreciated me like this."

And in a market like Los Angeles, we have a 0.1 percent unemployment rate in technology. So how does a government service, which pays less than the marketplace, compete in that environment? The power of the written word is the tool we use. I recently had to fill five vacancies in this highly competitive technology area. When I put out the recruitment posting, I had 430 applicants to choose from. I credit this to the reputation we have created. The word gets out about how people are treated and appreciated here. And again, it's all from the power of the written word.

Dean incorporates trust, education, and appreciation into his retention and recruitment initiatives. The results are inspiring, to say the least.

What it all really comes down to is the power of human connection. No matter where the human race resides, we want to feel connection. We all fill various roles in our lives; employer, employee, customer, friend, spouse, sibling, parent, child. We all fill these roles, but we never stop being a human being who wants to feel connection.

Remember this next time you walk through the office where your home team resides. Derek Brown felt a connection with Gregg Bryars, a senior vice president who took the time to recognize him as a human, not as a janitor. Dean Gialamas has employees who keep the greeting cards he has sent them on their shelves for years. The managers and employees at my company have cards hanging on their walls from their bosses, their co-workers, and even the customers they serve.

Why? Because everyone craves human connection. We simply want to be trusted, we want to learn, and we want to feel appreciated. If we have those things, we are generally happier, more productive, and we have more of a desire to be better at sending out those things to others.

Take care of the home team and the home team will take care of you. It's that simple. You will generate more new business, retain more of your existing business, and be more profitable if you work as a team.

SECTION 3

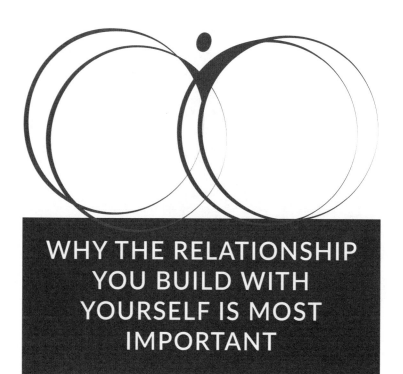

WHY THE RELATIONSHIP YOU BUILD WITH YOURSELF IS MOST IMPORTANT

CHAPTER 12

Creating and Building Your Personal Brand

n chapter 1, we talked about the three core principles that make up a strong relationship marketing plan.

Core Principle #1

Develop your personal brand and build it with friendship, celebration, and service.

Core Principle #2

Relationship first, 80 percent of the time.
Marketing second, 20 percent of the time.

Core Principle #3

Master the bridge between high-tech and personal touch.

Throughout this book we have discussed, with examples and stories, the second and third principles. I want to circle back now to the first principle. It's actually here where everything starts, but to leverage what the marketplace wants from us, we give you the other principles first.

The marketplace wants to know what relationship marketing is and how they can leverage it to increase sales, retain business, and generate referrals. We have given you countless examples of this in action. But to leverage those things to their fullest capacity, you need to begin with the relationship within. Your own personal development is critical to what you have to offer the marketplace.

To create human connection you need to nourish what's on the inside so you can send out the best version of what you have to offer the world. What you offer can be defined as your personal brand. You simply want to find out who you are so you can give yourself away to the world. And remember, what you send out is what you get back.

I believe every human being has unique, God-given gifts and talents. Each of us has a potential within us that is incomprehensible. We are meant to do amazing, glorious, and wonderful things in our life. We are also tempted, in this negative cynical world, to sell ourselves short, to give into limitation and doubt, to believe in the lie that we are not enough or that someone else gets all the breaks.

You will notice I just mentioned two opposite directions that pull at our minds and souls on a daily basis. This is illustrated in the story of a Cherokee grandfather who was teaching his grandson about life, using the metaphor of two wolves fighting within—one evil, and one good. His grandson asked, "Which wolf will win?" And the grandfather replied, "The one you feed the most."

I hope you can see this is karma working within you. What you send to yourself with thoughts, beliefs, actions, and habits is what you become. And the person you have created within is what you are sending out to others.

You might be asking how this relates to your relationship marketing plan. Well, it's the very thing that feeds that plan. Without it, there is nothing to offer. What you are feeding most within is what becomes your personal brand; it is how the world sees you.

YOUR PERSONAL BRAND

In your life and in your business, people **buy into you**. They **make a connection** with you. They establish a **relationship** with you. They build an **emotional attachment** to you. Ultimately, they buy into your **personal brand**.

Your personal brand is your purpose presentation. Remember, the key to mastering relationships is to find out who you are (your purpose) so you can give yourself away (your presentation). It's not enough to know who you are presently; you must find out who you are meant to be. If you are going to give yourself away, make sure it is the best version of you. The best version of you is the you that is on-purpose.

FINDING YOU

Your thoughts, beliefs, and habits make up who you are. They also determine what you can accomplish. Everything begins with your thoughts. What you are thinking about and how it makes you feel is what you become. You can have off-purpose thoughts that lead to negative beliefs and habits, or you can have on-purpose thoughts that lead to positive beliefs and habits.

- Off-purpose thoughts come from our world environment where 87 percent of everything you are exposed to is negative.

- On-purpose thoughts come from you and the environment you choose.
- Off-purpose thoughts tell you what you can't do.
- On-purpose thoughts tell you what you can, should, and will do.

Your thoughts turn into stories, and the stories in your mind become the stories of your life.

CREATING ON-PURPOSE STORIES IN YOUR MIND THAT SERVE YOU

You start by creating "I am" statements. These are simple, positive statements of things you desire. You want to begin these statements with the words, "I am."

We do this because our subconscious mind does not know the difference between what is real and what is imagined. If you send out a message in present tense, starting with the words "I am," your subconscious mind believes it, acts upon it, and delivers whatever you send it.

Your goal is to create your on-purpose statements and make them more dominant in your life than your off-purpose statements. You end up living your most dominant statements whether you believe you do or not.

THE KEY WORD IS DOMINANT

Let's say you are a real estate agent, you want to sell 50 homes in one year, and you want your primary source of leads to come from referral. You write an "I am" statement that says, "I am selling 50 homes a year, all from referrals." If that becomes your most dominant thought, then the manifestation process begins. You will consciously start doing the fundamentals that bring you more referrals.

Here is the challenge, and it happens to most people who write statements like this. They have written down and often read the words, "I am selling 50 homes a year all from referrals." But, then, without even knowing it, in their daily language they are saying or thinking things like, "Who am I kidding? I'm never going to sell 50 homes in one year. People are not going to go out of their way to give me referrals. The market is turning for the worse. The mortgage rules are messed up so people can't get qualified."

And on and on go their thoughts and their daily language. And the worst part is, they don't even know they are doing it. Their daily language becomes more dominant than the statements that were written down. Those thoughts eat away at their daily actions until they are no longer doing the fundamentals consistently enough to give them results. They are not making karma their niche. To them, karma just became a you know what!

You see how this works. You've already heard a story about one of my students, Gayle Zientek. She is a real estate agent and first attended one of my events in 2008. Keep in mind, the housing market had just crashed back then and she was seeking to improve her real estate closings. She went through our "I am" statement exercise and wrote down, among many others, these statements:

> *I am closing 50 homes per year by referral.*
> *I am in the top 5 percent of producing agents on our association board.*
> *I am attracting referrals to my business.*

One of the things that impressed me about Gayle is that she was an amazing student. She was committed to implementing what she was learning about relationship marketing and manifesting those statements into her life. She wrote those statements and she went to work. She became a master at relationship marketing.

Her goal was to connect with 50 people per day using social media, networking events, and greeting cards. She also committed to having at least three conversations a day via texting, private messaging, and phone calls with new people in her network. She was moving them from her cool market to her warm market.

Gayle became a master at following people on social media and sending them lifestyle celebration cards in the mail. She attended networking events and did the same thing there. You may recall her story about sending a card to the guy who won the cook-off in her hometown. Gayle was really consistent with those things until they became unconscious activities. She became habitually consistent with those fundamentals. Within three years, she manifested each of her "I am" statements. She has consistently sold over 50 homes per year, all by referral, over the past four years.

I share these two scenarios to explain that most people fall into the first category. Their "I am" statements did not fail them; they failed their "I am" statements. Gayle did not fail her "I am" statements because she kept them dominant and she worked consistently until her actions became habits. That's how winning is done. That is how you make human connections. You keep sending out the thoughts, and doing the actions and the habits necessary to have your desired goal come back to you.

In our relationship marketing courses, we have people write down a list of as many "I am" statements as they can. And then we have them drill down to one core statement that represents all of them. We call this your "core purpose statement." This is the statement that defines who you are in one short sentence.

I have a long list of "I am" statements and finally drilled down to one core purpose statement that says, "I bring the human race together." After reading this book or hearing me speak, or even speaking to me on the phone, you will pick up on this with the stories I tell and the things I say. It is who I am. It is my personal brand.

Yes, the relationship marketing product I represent is cool and I'm obviously excited about it. But my why goes much deeper than just helping people succeed in business. I envision a world where people embrace their differences and come together as one human race. I leverage what the marketplace wants, which is a way to increase business and make money. I inspire them on what they need, which is a way to reach out and be nice to each other. That's what I get really excited about.

Gayle Zientek drilled down on all her statements and came up with one core purpose statement that said, "I am friendship, celebration, and service." That has resonated in everything she has done for the past 10 years. She is all about creating friendships with people she meets, celebrating their accomplishments, and providing exceptional service to people. By the way, she recently won the Realtor of the Year award in Kalamazoo, Michigan.

Keep in mind, the best way to create human connection is to find the best version of you, nourish that version of you, and give it away to the world. That is how you want the world to see you. Remember, people do business with those they know, like, and trust. You were meant to be the best version of yourself. Lots of people will know, like, and trust the best version of you. People like to be around those who are happy, confident, giving, and caring. When you are on-purpose, you naturally become those things.

CHAPTER 13

Shifting Karma to the Positive in Your Life

T here is a time-tested statement in marketing that says, "Fear of loss is a bigger motivator than the desire for gain." We have already displayed how this works when you present your products and services. Speaking to people's pain is essential to any good sales presentation.

Fear of losing something is the biggest pain of all. That's why you see advertising like:

- Limited time offer! If you don't buy now, you will lose out.
- If you don't buy our weight loss product, you will get fat.
- If you don't get life insurance, your family could be left behind and not taken care of.
- If you don't buy this investment today, you won't enjoy the potential returns.
- Get in on the ground floor or get left behind.

We can make a long list of examples where marketers use fear of loss as the motivator. I have never liked this about marketing, and in fact, for years I tried to defy the odds and ignore using that method with my companies. I figured we could inspire people on the need to send positivity and appreciation with cards and gifts. I was thinking we could ignore any need for fear of loss and only focus on the desire for gain.

This is what I didn't realize: the vast majority of the market-place is made of people who live in fear. That is why the fear of loss method works so well when you market products and services to them. This is also why lots of people associate the word "karma" as negative. If you are living in fear, you attract what you fear. The vibrational energy of fear is extremely low, and that energy becomes your karma.

....

Karma is nothing more than cause and effect.

What you send out comes back to you.

....

If your fear-based energy is low, then what you send out in thoughts, words, and deeds will have low energy (the cause). What happens next is you attract that same energy back to you (the effect). You often hear people say, "Why do bad things keep happening to me?" This is why.

So what is the opposite of fear? Fear is defined as "A distressing emotion aroused by impending danger, evil, pain, etc., whether the threat is real or imagined; the feeling or condition of being afraid." As I read that definition I can't help but think that in my own life, the word "faith" seems have the opposite effect. How do I define faith? With the help of the Bible, I would say, "Faith is the substance of things hoped for and the evidence of things not seen." The definition of fear says that fear is a threat of something painful that can be real or imagined. The definition of faith says that faith is a hope of something desired that can be real or imagined.

I learned a lot about faith from my father, not necessarily by what he said but by how he lived his life. My dad was an entrepreneur who owned his own electrical contracting company. Over the years, he employed anywhere from two to 40 people.

He had to deal with the ebbs and flows of the economy, collection issues that choked his cash flow, and unexpected twists and turns with employees, suppliers, and customers. You name the challenge and I watched him go through it. And that was just his business. We had a large family and dad seemed to always be there to take care of everybody.

My dad simply believed his way through every challenge that life brought him. He lived a happy life. He was always positive and he always seemed to come out on top. My dad also cared deeply about people. He loved people. He accepted you for who you were, whether he agreed with you or not. It was the faith he had and the love he shared that made him a winner in life. I remember him saying, "Things always have their way of working out." He just lived that way. He made powerful human connections, and it worked for him and for us as a family.

I am also an entrepreneur. I have experienced the same ebbs and flows of owning my own companies. There have been many times where I had to rely upon that same kind of faith to see us through challenging times. Those words, "Things always have their way of working out," have been branded in my mind, my heart, and my soul. They have seen me through seemingly impossible challenges. Following the example of my father, "the desire for gain" has been the driving motivation for most of my life.

With most people fear of loss is a bigger motivator than the desire for gain. Here is the challenge with this: the motivation you have chosen is where you reside. So if fear is a bigger motivator, then fear is where you reside. If faith is a bigger motivator, then faith is where you reside.

If you want to shift karma to the positive in your life, then you want to reside on the "desire for gain" side more than you do on the "fear of loss" side. To do this requires a conscious shift, where you consciously think about the desired shift you seek.

MAKING FAITH (DESIRE FOR GAIN) THE MOTIVATOR OVER FEAR (FEAR OF LOSS)

I believe there are four powerful ways to make this shift:

1. *Have to* versus *want to*
2. Problem versus challenge
3. Sacrifice versus opportunity
4. Anti versus pro

1. *Have to* versus *want to*

One of the best ways to make this shift is to begin doing things because you *want to*, not because you *have to*.

Do you work out because you *have to* or because you *want to*?

Do you diet because you *have to* or because you *want to*?

Do you budget or invest because you *have to* or because you *want to*?

Do you pay tithes because you *have to* or because you *want to*?

Do you go to church because you *have to* or because you *want to*?

Are you nice to people because you *have to* or because you *want to*?

Do you send appreciation to your prospects and customers because you feel like you *have to* or because you *want to*?

What would you have on your own list of *have to* versus *want to* things in your life?

Why is this important?

When you feel like you *have to* do something, you are coming from a place of fear (fear of loss). When you *want to* do something you are coming from a place of faith (desire for gain).

I *have to* work out because I don't want to be overweight and look bad, versus I *want to* diet because it makes me feel good.

I *have to* budget and invest my money because I don't want to lose it, versus I *want to* budget and invest my money because compounded interest will make me wealthy.

I *have to* follow up with my customers or they will move their business, versus I *want to* follow up with my customers because I care about them.

This is the kind of shift that gets you into the faith-based "desire for gain" side of living.

Is it bad to feel like you "have to" do things?

I remember teaching this concept in a church Sunday school class once. We were talking about the *have to* versus *want to* list that was associated with our church.

Do I go to church because I *have to* or because I *want to*?

Do I pay tithes and offerings because I *have to* or because I *want to*?

The group I was teaching was an older group of people. They were long-time active members of the church. They were really getting into this conversation until I posed a question: "If I leave this room and walk down the hall of this church to the classroom where your teenage kids are, and I say to them, 'You should not come to church because you have to, you should come to church because you want to.' How is that going to make you feel?"

Wow, did the conversation shift in a hurry! As you can imagine, many of those parents had to drag their teenage kids to church that day, because how many teenage kids want to go to church over lounging at home on a lazy Sunday morning?

The point of this story is that it's not bad to feel like you have to do things. In fact, it is necessary in the beginning. There is a conversion process that takes place when you adopt new activities in your life.

I don't think anybody wants to run on a treadmill at the gym until they are ready to throw up or pass out. But they do it because they feel like they have to at first. That motivation got them started. If that *have to* motivation continues, however, chances are that person stops running on the treadmill. At some point, the earlier the better, the conversion or the shift from *have to* over to *want to* needs to take place. That is the shift that keeps you going. It's the shift that gives you the right attitude and energy. It's how you shift karma to the positive side of your life.

2. Problem versus challenge:

Problem: This is a negative word and is related directly to fear of loss.

Challenge: This is a motivation word and is related directly to desire for gain.

I own companies that rely heavily on technology. We have programmers who have an ongoing need to maintain a highly sophisticated system while they develop new systems. You can imagine that this comes with its inherent set of ongoing problems. I remember going to the office, and before I could sit behind my desk, I would be hit with a new set of problems for the day. It got to the point where the word "problem" was the dominant word around the office. We noticed that energy became low, morale was challenged, and people at the office were on edge. When you focus on something as a problem, you seem to attract more problems. Remember, karma is all about cause and effect.

I decided that I was no longer going to allow myself or anyone at the office to say the word "problem," and all together, we replaced the word "problem" with the word "challenge." This was not easy to do. It took time but it created a dramatic shift in how we approached things.

Challenge is a motivation word. It generates the competitive spirit that seems to be in all of us. It implies that if we overcome the challenge we gain our desired results. My challenge to you is to get rid of the word "problem" in your life and replace it with the word "challenge."

3. Sacrifice versus opportunity:

Sacrifice: This is a negative word and implies you must lose something to gain something.

Opportunity: This is a positive word that focuses on the side of gaining something.

We have all heard people say things like, "If you sacrifice spending money today you will have money to spend for a lifetime," and, "If you sacrifice one extra hour of sleep in the morning you will have more time to accomplish your goals."

I'm not saying those statements are not true, because they are. However, they imply or pay attention to the idea that you have to give something up to gain what you want. That kind of focus keeps you in a place of fear of loss. Opportunity, on the other hand, means the same thing, but keeps you in a place of desire for gain.

Now I hear people say things like, "I have an opportunity to save and invest money today and it will provide me with money to spend for a lifetime," and, "I have the opportunity to wake up one hour earlier every day. It actually gives me more energy and extra time to accomplish my goals." That kind of focus keeps you in a place of desire for gain.

4. Anti versus pro:

We live in a day and age where everyone seems to be passionate about their causes and are hypercritical of the things they don't support. To me, it just makes more sense to stay focused on being *pro* something instead of *anti* anything.

The challenge is bigger than ever before because social media gives us a place to post our views and read the views of others; I believe social media is a big reason for the division we see in our society today. People always had strong views on one side or the other of the issues we are debating today. The difference now is that we post them for the whole world to see. Because of this, the debates are bigger and nastier than ever before. The challenge is that all of this creates really bad energy—the kind that makes karma a bitch, not your niche.

I believe the solution is simple. Focus your energies on being pro something instead of bashing against the opposite side of your cause. Don't read this and make it political. The purpose of this chapter is to get you to shift into the desire for gain side of things.

> If you focus on what you are for, you will accomplish that shift. If you focus on what you are against, you will not accomplish that shift, because you are fighting with your fear of loss.

To shift karma to the positive side of your life, you need to stay positive. I have outlined some powerful ways for you to do this. With karma on the positive side you can do amazing things with your personal brand. You will naturally build your brand with friendship, celebration, and service. And it will be easier for you to master the relationship marketing strategies I have outlined throughout this book.

CHAPTER 14

How to Leverage the Law of Attraction

The law of attraction is karma in action. It simply means that what you send out in life is what comes back to you (cause and effect). If you send out negative, you get negative results. If you send out positive, you get positive results.

We have already mentioned that 87 percent of everything you take in is negative and becomes the ultimate challenge.

The solution to that challenge:

1. Flush the negative out.
2. Replace with positive-in.
3. Send out the positives to the world.
4. Receive what you send tenfold.

FLUSH THE NEGATIVE OUT

This is a daily routine. You have to find ways to flush out negativity because you will be exposed to it. The first thing that is essential to this is to minimize the negativity you expose yourself to. As an example, I'm not a fan of watching the news or listening to controversial talk shows. It is important to stay informed and get involved with issues you have a passion for. We all just need to be careful what we expose ourselves to.

Rather than watching or listening to 30-minute or 60-minute segments of news, subscribe to a news blog of choice and scan it quickly. This way, you can be informed on community, country and world events, and you can choose the stories you want to involve yourself with.

The negative-in vehicle that caught me off guard was social media. I had been scanning news feeds for several years before I realized they were having a negative impact on me. Don't take this wrong, I'm a firm believer of being active on social media, but only in positive, production-building ways.

Limit the time you spend as an observer on social media. Spend more time contributing than you do scrolling. If you feel negative emotion from someone's post or comments, that's a good time to put your smartphone down.

REPLACE WITH POSITIVE-IN

Listen to positive downloads and read personal development and business books. If you like fiction, then add good fiction books to your list. I have already mentioned that reading has always been one of my saving graces. It's the very thing that allowed me to enhance the environment I was raised in. I was reminded of this when I recently went to lunch with my niece Andrea. Our family is large and highly diversified, and Andrea said, "You and all your brothers and sisters grew up in the same home. You all had the same influence with your mom and dad. How did you all turn out so different?"

"It has to do with what we all exposed ourselves to," I answered. "I can't speak for my siblings, but I attribute who I am and where I am today based on the books I have read." I went on to explain that, fortunately for me, my mother (her grandmother) put me in an accelerated reading course when I was five years old. I acquired a love of reading at a very early age.

At the age of 15, I was introduced to my first personal development book, *How to Win Friends and Influence People* by Dale Carnegie. I loved that book and soon learned there were more books like it. I started buying and reading them one at a time. Before I knew it, I had built a library of books from Dale Carnegie, Norman Vincent Peale, Og Mandino, and other influential positive personal development authors. Over the years, I have accumulated a library of over 2,000 books. When you read three to four books a month consistently over 40 years, that turns into a lot of books.

That conversation with my niece made me realize just how much those books have influenced my life. I'm sure the knowledge I've gained from those books have made karma a positive word in my life.

SEND OUT POSITIVES TO THE WORLD

This is why having a relationship system is so important. I have dedicated my entire professional career to creating products and services that help me and others send out positivity to the world. Simply put, just be nice to people. Smile at them, make eye contact, say hello, open the door for people, be considerate, let people in when you're in traffic, call someone just to say hi, and send unexpected cards to people.

RECEIVE WHAT YOU SEND OUT TENFOLD

What this suggests is that whatever you are sending out will come back to you tenfold. I joke with people at my seminars by asking them how much tenfold is. A few always try to explain exactly what tenfold means, but I always conclude by saying, "It's a **whole bunch**." So this means that if you send out kindness, then more kindness than what you sent will come back to you.

The same thing applies to anything you are sending out. There is one activity that will accomplish all four of these things in less than two minutes a day. We call it becoming a *level-four card sender*. Make it a goal.

If you remember, level four is called unconscious competence, when you no longer think about an activity, you just do it. Level four is when the activity becomes a habit. Think about it. If you did nothing more than send a heartfelt greeting card every day, you would flush negativity out, replace it with positive-in, send out the positives to the world, and begin receiving what you send out tenfold. Every day.

When you are typing or writing words of kindness to another human being, it is not possible to think of anything negative at the same time.

You have those few minutes of undivided attention on being positive. And you are sending that positivity out at the same time.

SENDING OUT TO GIVE

You give yourself away by sending out your **thoughts, feelings, words, and deeds.** When you send a written message to someone, you have the thought behind the message. That thought evokes emotions or feelings you have for that person. You translate your thoughts and feelings into words that you type or write, and then, with systems like mine, you click "send" and the deed is complete. As the famous quote says, at the end of the day, it's not what you say or do that matters; it's how you make people feel.

Think about this the next time you want to reach out to a prospect or customer. They don't care what your deal is nearly as much as they care about how much you care. When you make a customer, friend, family member, or significant other feel appreciated, they will move to the end of the world and back for you.

So when you are sending out your thoughts, feelings, words, and deeds to others, I want to ask you an important question: Are you sending out to *get* from them? Or are you sending out to *give* to them?

The law of attraction says if you are sending out to get, meaning you want something from the person you are sending to, then the universe will get, or possibly take away from you. Does that sound weird? Let's go back to the story I shared in an earlier chapter about Hugh Thompson, the State Farm Insurance guy. His corporate office was sending out the form letter, on State Farm letterhead, in a form letter format, asking for business and referrals, and signed by Hugh Thompson with his picture on it.

His response to this letter is ZERO. Nothing. In fact his customers, prospects, and friends throw that letter in the trash and do not have a warm and fuzzy feeling about Hugh when they do it. This is an example of the universe running the other way.

The law of attraction also says if you are sending out to give, meaning you want only to give something to the person you are sending to, then the universe will give to you. If you remember, Hugh Thompson later sent out a personalized card to the girls' basketball team. Again, there was nothing about State Farm anywhere on the card. Hugh was simply building a relationship. He was not asking anything of the coach, Jerry. He was simply celebrating Jerry's life and his great accomplishment. Hugh understands the importance of building relationships. Now, what do you suppose Jerry will do when he or anyone he knows has insurance needs? This is an example of the universe giving back.

This is not just some crazy new age philosophy about the supply of the universe. These examples show you the concept in action. To further illustrate the power of this concept, I want you to visualize how humanity is different and how humanity is the same. If you can learn to channel your energies on how we are naturally the same, it becomes much easier to embrace how we are all different.

HOW WE ARE ALL DIFFERENT AND HOW WE ARE ALL THE SAME

The highest level of positive energy is created when we place the same value on others as we place on ourselves. This is where good karma comes from. We can focus on how we are all different or we can focus on how we are the same. If we focus on our differences and try to *get* other people to become like us, we lose energy and karma begins to work against us. If we focus on how we are the same and strive to *give* to others what we are all seeking, then we gain energy and karma works for us.

To illustrate, let's first talk about how we are all different. Below you will notice two windows. One is dark gray and one is light gray. These are what we call *value and belief windows.*

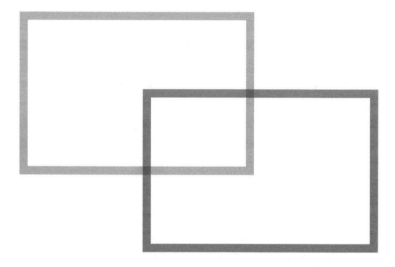

Let's say the light gray one is my value and belief window and the dark gray one is your value and belief window. Where they overlap is the area where you and I think, feel, and act the same way. We might have some of the same interests and beliefs and we might even value some things the same. These are things we have in common. This is how we create interest in each other and carry on cheerful conversation.

Outside the overlap area is where we are different. The top left side is where I think, feel, and act totally different than you do, and the bottom right side is where you think, feel, and act totally differently than I do. What happens if you or I try to get these value and belief windows to perfectly align or even more closely align? There is actually nothing we can do to make that happen.

This same thing applies to any relationship you have in your life. Do this with your spouse, your children, your friends, or neighbors. It doesn't matter. We all have our own window and we are never going to force someone else's window to align with our own.

Now think about what is going on in the world today. How often do we see people attacking differences instead of embracing them? Because of social media, we are exposed to others' value and belief windows, and we want to debate our differences. This is what causes separation. It's not politicians or world leaders that are separating us. This is what separates us. If you want to make genuine human connections, you need to embrace differences, not attack them.

Below is a slightly altered version of the value and belief windows. This time there are some dotted lines that give it the appearance of a box. The first thing I would like you to do is write "common interests" in the small box where the windows overlap. Notice also that there are four lines at the top and bottom cor-

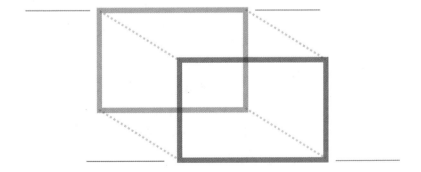

ners of the box. I would like you to write the following words on each of those lines:

Race   Gender
Values   Beliefs

And finally, I would like you to trace over the dotted lines. Why did I have you do this? We already know that the overlap represents our common interests. The four words represent the four general areas where we are different. We were born into the world with race and gender. We learned values and beliefs as we have journeyed through life.

I'm sure you could list more than 100 ways we have differences, including religion, politics, nationalities, lifestyle preference, etc. But all of them fall under one of those four master categories.

Tracing over the dotted lines represents our willingness to embrace those differences. It creates a perfect three-dimensional box that represents coming together. You will notice we did not slide the boxes to overlay each other. This would be an attempt to force alignment of values and beliefs. We have already established that is impossible. Instead, we drew lines of embracement. This allows you to continue to be you, and me to continue to be me.

Some of you might be saying that drawing those lines for real in our society today might be easier said than done. I'm going to show you a way where drawing those lines actually becomes very simple. We do it by focusing on how we are already the same with others. We are all the same in that we have a desire to love and be loved.

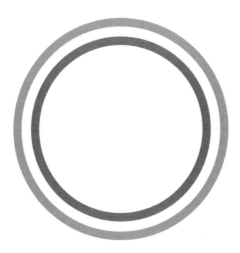

These two circles are naturally in alignment. That's because everyone who is breathing has this in common. If we simply focus on caring about others, being kind, sharing appreciation and creating connections, then judgment begins to fall by the wayside. Instead of focusing on differences, we actually embrace them, because now we are focused on how we all want to be embraced. This makes it easy to draw those lines up above.

I want to be with people who are different than I am. My life is immensely blessed because I am able to see things in so many different ways. Some of my closest friends, people whom I would consider family, are from different races, religions, nationalities, lifestyle preferences, and viewpoints. We live in a higher sphere of energy—not because we are better than anyone else, but because we place the same value on others as we place on ourselves.

One of the things I love about our relationship marketing systems is they teach people how to embrace others. Most people start using them because they want better results in their business, and that's OK. We are simply leveraging what you want from us, which is a system that generates referral and repeat business.

But in the process of using the system and learning the philosophies outlined in this book, you begin to be inspired on what you need from our systems. That is a way to reach out in kindness to others, a way to embrace people's differences, and a way to bring people together.

If you recall, my core purpose statement that represents my personal brand is, "I bring the human race together." I simply cannot write this book about relationship marketing without having that message brought out loud and clear. If you want to master the positive side of karma, simply embrace these time-tested personal development principles.

CHAPTER 15

A Mindset for Abundance and Prosperity

Most people live in scarcity, constantly worried if they will have enough, with many living the "too much month at the end of the paycheck" experience. Or is it a mindset?

As I've mentioned, what you send out is what comes back to you. If you are in a state of lack and limitation, then you attract lack and limitation. This mindset is a challenge when you are striving to create human connection or when you're striving to be in a constant state of giving. When I mention having a "give for the sake of giving philosophy," this means you serve others any way you can, whenever you can, without concern for what's in it for you. When you're in a mindset of "lack," this becomes difficult to do.

I remember an experience I had with one of my motorcycle mechanics several years ago, when the social media craze was just taking off. I was the perfect type of customer for this guy, because I didn't have time to do my own wrenching. But I like to have my motor vehicles serviced and ready to go when I have the time to use them. However, there were times when the things I needed done were quick and simple fixes. I thought, "Wouldn't it be nice If I could go somewhere on the internet and learn how to do some of this stuff?"

I said to my mechanic, "You should create a blog or website about motorcycle mechanics. You could have a list of most common questions with answers on how to fix things. You could even video record demonstrations."

I will never forget the way he looked at me. You would have thought I just suggested the stupidest idea in the world. He said, "Why would I ever do that? Customers come in to my shop and ask me all the time how to fix things."

"Well, it sounds like that's even more reason why you should do it," I said. "With the internet and social media and YouTube, people are going to start looking online for solutions anyway. You might as well be the first expert they see." Keep in mind, this was before you could search YouTube for any topic you could imagine and see a video on how to do it.

This mechanic was excellent at what he did, one of the best I have ever known. Instead of embracing the concept of giving away his expertise on social media, he got frustrated with it. He ended up closing his shop and went into another line of work.

Today, there are countless stories of people who give away their knowledge for free on the internet. Most of those people have thriving businesses that sell the very services they give away. How does that work? Because what you send out comes back to you. With social media and the internet, you now have tools where you can give away your knowledge like never before.

Those who share their knowledge are well-liked by people who benefit from their selfless assistance. And guess what happens? Those same people call you when they need your service, and they refer others to you.

The days of hoarding your knowledge and expertise are over. The more you give away today, the more business you will receive. More than ever before, it is essential that you shift from a mindset of scarcity to a mindset of abundance.

MAKING THE SHIFT

First, we need to explore the concept of abundance. The universe we reside in is a universe of abundance. Our world is a world of abundance.

I want you to imagine laying on a beautiful, freshly cut lawn. Keep your eyes open and focus on the individual blades of grass. Look closely. How many blades of grass are on your front lawn alone? Try it—you will be amazed. We are talking millions of blades of grass in a small yard. Multiply that by the millions of lawns there are around the world, and that's a whole lot of blades of grass. You can do this with anything. Look at a tree, any tree that's in full bloom. How many leaves are on that tree? How many pine needles are on a single pine tree?

I'm writing this in February while in flight from San Diego, California, to Salt Lake City, Utah. We flew out to the west and made a gradual turn over the Pacific Ocean. As we made that turn, I looked out at the ocean. For as far as I could see there was water. I could also see ripples in the water caused by the tides—millions of lines in the water representing waves, millions of waves.

We flew northeast. A large snowstorm had just hit the western states. As far as I could see, in every direction, it was white with snow. The mountains and valley floors were covered with snow for hundreds of miles in every direction. In some places, it looked like several feet of snow had just fallen. How did that snow get there? One flake at a time; trillions and trillions of unique snowflakes falling gracefully to the ground.

Go into the wilderness at night where the city lights do not obstruct your view. Look into the sky and you see millions and millions of stars. And those are just stars you can see! I am told there are millions of galaxies of stars that we cannot see even with high-powered telescopes.

This is a whole lot of evidence that all the creations and laws of nature in the universe come from a place of abundance. There is also evidence that, of all those creations, the greatest creation of all is a human being. Each of us is a breathing, speaking, thinking, feeling, self-healing, procreating creation, and we love, care, create, and make a difference in that same universe that is so abundant. So if we, the greatest of all of God's creations, live within a universe of nothing but abundance, how is it that we place lack and limitation on ourselves?

I want you to really think about this. It's good to go through an exercise like this because it helps us to think more from a state of abundance. Everything in our world and in our universe thrives on the laws of abundance. That includes YOU!

....

You do not have to be abundant to attract abundance, but you do have to feel abundance.

....

Any feeling of lack of abundance causes a mindset that does not allow abundance. If you feel abundance, you will send out to yourself and others to give. If you feel a lack of abundance, you will send out to yourself and to others to get.

Lack and limitation is not natural; it's made up. And it will move you away from the natural laws of abundance. Abundance is the natural law. If you think it and feel it and work at it, you will become it. If you focus on the abundance around you and create a statement like, "I am abundance and prosperity," then the laws of karma begin to attract abundance toward you. At some of my events I have suggested writing a list of "I am" statements that are focused on abundance and prosperity.

That list might include statements like:

I am ever blessed with divine rights of abundance and prosperity.

I bring blessings and goodwill to all that I come in contact with.

I am a source of acceptance.

I am my own greatest blessing.

I am positivity, and therefore attract all that is positive.

I am a money magnet and attract ongoing financial increase.

I enjoy a life of abundance.

My business delivers immense value to the marketplace.

My business receives, acquires, and delivers new possibilities.

My business generates an abundant supply of cash and profits.

I leverage ongoing cash flow to maximize financial increase.

My ever-increasing wealth is used to bring massive opportunity to those who are less fortunate.

I wish the blessings of abundance and prosperity on all people who desire it.

*I accept others' abilities to use their blessings as their values
    see fit.*

*I enjoy an abundant supply of faith, which brings an ongoing
    increase of possibility.*

In addition to specific statements built around the words of
abundance and prosperity, I also wrote statements that were
merely related to the concept of abundance and prosperity.
Each of those statements conveys abundance principles that we
should briefly explore.

Being a source of acceptance

Because the universe is abundant, that universe (or whatever
higher power you believe in) is designed to shower its blessings
upon you. The biggest blockage to those blessings is you. When
you feel you are not worthy, or not good enough, or not deserving, or are simply stuck in a mindset of lack, you don't accept the
blessing when it comes your way. When you say, "I am a source
of acceptance," you open the doors for blessings and new possibilities to flow your way.

Being your own greatest blessing

This is simply a statement of truth. Many of you from a reli-
gious or faith-based persuasion may be questioning what I just
said. Before you get emotionally worked up over it, please understand what I mean. Many of you (including me) believe blessings
come from God or a higher power. Others believe differently.

Regardless of where you believe the source is, you have to
work in conjunction with that source to accept, leverage, and
make a difference with that blessing. So when you say, "I am my

own greatest blessing," you are saying you and whatever source you believe in controls your destiny. You don't rely on fate or other people or anything other than yourself and your source to generate those blessings.

Being positive and attracting positivity

Abundance is positivity in action. Lack and limitation is negativity in action. Because of this, positivity springs from an abundant mindset, and positivity is available in abundance so you can attract an unlimited supply of positivity in your life.

Being a money magnet

Many studies have been conducted to determine which words in the English language provoke the most emotion, good or bad. High on every tester's list is the word "money." The reason the word "money" generates such high emotion is because either people don't have enough of it (negative emotion), or the thought of money gets them excited about what they can do with it (positive emotion).

Saying "I am a money magnet" implies that money will flow to you and there is an abundant supply. You want to find yourself feeling a positive emotion every time you hear the word "money."

Generating an abundant supply of cash and profits

This is designed more for your business. Cash flow and profitability are the two biggest factors to success (and also to stress) when it comes to running a business. By saying, "I am generating an abundant supply of cash and profits," you are sending out that your business is thriving. You are saying there is abundant possibility for increased cash flow and profits that generate opportunity for wealth and reinvestment.

Providing immense value to the marketplace

Your financial worth is directly proportionate to the value you offer the marketplace. If your mindset is to provide immense value, then you will naturally embrace relationship marketing principles; you will think of your value in terms of "immense" or abundant, and you will have a constant desire to deliver immense value. The result is an immense increase in financial worth.

Providing opportunity for those who are less fortunate

This focuses on the need to give back to the communities and experiences from whence you came. The concept of giving back puts you in the mindset of serving your fellow human beings. Because you are an abundant being, you have an abundance of time, care and expertise to reach out, despite how busy you are, to help others along the way.

Accepting others' right to use their blessings in the way they choose

Judging how other people live their lives implies there is a limited supply of what those people should do with their lives. And usually people who feel this way also believe their way of life is all there is. Because there is an abundant supply of needs, wants, desires, and values in the world today, we should realize there is no need for everyone to agree with us or have a passion for how we see the world. These are all added principles that will help in your quest to build strong relationships as you build your human connections.

When you make these statements, remember you are sending these messages to your subconscious. The subconscious mind does not think; it feels. You do not have to be abundance. You just need to feel abundance to attract abundance. And no, I am not saying that you sit in your closet and sing abundance affirmations to yourself all day. I'm saying your thoughts and your language need to create an abundance mindset. With that mindset, you go out and do the work. Implement the things you've learned in this book. Think bigger, think better, work harder, and work smarter.

THE WEALTHY MINDSET

As we progress daily with creating an abundance and prosperity mindset, we can specifically channel that mindset into creating wealth. Wealthy people simply think, feel, and act differently than non-wealthy people. They have a different mindset. They typically hang out with other wealthy people. Their discussions are different and their thought processes are different.

This reminds me of an experience I had doing a seminar many years ago. We were at the Marina Del Ray Hotel in Marina Del Ray, California. This hotel was right on the water. Our meeting room looked over the boat docks where beautiful sailboats and motor yachts rested in their slips. In this room we had big windows along the outer wall where you could look out and see the marina in full view. The scent of the ocean was delivered by a cool breeze, and you could take it all in as you stepped outside the meeting room onto a deck overlooking the water. This was a perfect location for an incredible event.

Southern California is truly an amazing place, a land with sunshine, blue skies, sandy ocean beaches, and a world of abundance all around you. You see it in the lifestyles and attitudes of the people you meet there. At the Marina Del Ray event, we did a wealthy-mindset exercise with those in attendance. This is a simple exercise that defines how wealthy people think, feel, and act. We made it through this exercise in record time. Why? Because, the people in attendance already had a wealth-building mindset. At other events around the world we spend lots of time discussing these concepts because people don't understand them. Not in So-Cal. This is truly a land of abundance. Do you think it's a coincidence that you see so much prosperity there? I don't think so, because there is a different mindset there.

My family came with me to this event. We flew into Newport Beach and drove down to the Newport Bay area to have lunch at a place called the Rusty Pelican. We pulled up to the valet and made our way into the restaurant. There was a line of exotic cars parked close to the entryway that immediately got our attention. I specifically remember seeing a new Aston Martin and a Phantom Rolls Royce parked next to each other. At the time, I had teenage kids, and let me tell you, their eyes were popping out of their heads. When we sat in the Rusty Pelican, we looked around and observed the people who were dining there. We couldn't hear their conversations but we didn't have to. We felt their energy, and it energized us! I like to find places like this and hang out there. Abundant thinking is contagious, and I want to be around it as much as I can.

WHAT DOES A WEALTHY MINDSET LOOK LIKE?

Wealthy people focus on their big picture or purpose. Poor people focus on their little pictures or daily routines.

Wealthy people focus on the long-term gain from their efforts. Poor people focus on their short-term results.

Wealthy people have a mindset for abundance. Poor people have a mindset for security or control.

Wealthy people go outside of their comfort zones. Poor people do all they can to protect their comfort zones.

Wealthy people never play the game of "victim." Poor people become a "victim" in most of their dealings. As T. Harv Eker says, "You can be a victim or you can be rich, but you can't be both."

Wealthy people learn and grow. Poor people think they know.

Wealthy people focus on their "why." Poor people focus on their "how."

Wealthy people spend time on personal development training. Poor people skip to the how-to training.

Wealthy people visualize what they desire. Poor people wonder how they will ever get what they desire.

Wealthy people leverage their time, talents, and money with relationships. Poor people guard their time, talent, and money with fear.

Wealthy people don't think about it, they do it. Poor people think and talk about it but don't do it.

Wealthy people celebrate the success of others. Poor people judge the success of others.

Wealthy people believe they can have their cake and eat it too. Poor people don't believe they deserve cake, so they order a doughnut, focus on the hole, and wonder why they have nothing.

Wealthy people know how to set their money blueprint. Poor people don't know they have a money blueprint.

Reading through my journal the other day, I came upon this passage: "I choose to celebrate every day by exploring new possibilities. I will not tear down; I will build up. I will not be critical; I will be productive. I will not be a pro at what is wrong; I will be a pro at what is right. I choose to stay in a creative mindset, always brainstorming, always exploring new opportunities, and always building. I will spend my time with those who do the same thing. 'Upward and onward' is the motto I choose to live by every day. I choose to live in abundance. I notice the beautiful blue sky, the abundance of leaves on the trees, the abundance of goodness in the world, the smiles instead of the frowns, the laughter and the feel-good emotions that are everywhere. I am a money magnet. I attract wealth in abundance because there is an abundant supply. I continually add value to the marketplace with who I am. I gladly share my wealth of knowledge, time, talent, and money with those who are in need. I had a starting point, and I was mentored along the way. I recognize everyone has a starting point, and I am there to give back that which was given to me. I celebrate the genius within everyone I meet. Talents, gifts, and abilities are flowing from the hearts and minds of everyone around me."

These are the thoughts that go through the mind of a wealth-conscious person. Everyone has the ability to think like this. When these thoughts come to you, write them down. You will cherish them forever.

One of my biggest heroes is Norman Vincent Peale. He said it like this: "We are here to be excited from youth to old age, to have an insatiable curiosity about the world. We are also here to help others by practicing a friendly attitude, and every person is born for a purpose. Everyone has a God-given potential, in essence, built into them, and if we are to live life to its fullest, we must realize that potential."

Now that you have the wealthy versus poor mindset fresh in your conscious thoughts, I want you to think again of abundance, its true meaning, and the law of cause and effect; what you send out is what comes back to you. Those who have created the wealthy mindset are on the positive side of karma when it comes to building wealth and experiencing an abundant lifestyle.

MONEY BLUEPRINT

Wealthy people know how to set their money blueprint. In his book *Secrets of the Millionaire Mind*, T. Harv Eker teaches us about money blueprints. I highly recommend you study his work. He says, "We all have a blueprint in our minds of how much we are worth or how much money we can expect to make We make whatever that blueprint is."

Take a person who is used to making $5,000 per month and then loses her source of income. When a new source of income shows up, it doesn't take long before she is back to $5,000 per month. Her money blueprint is set at $5,000 per month.

Those who have challenges with money usually don't know anything about having a money blueprint. That doesn't mean they don't have one. Their preconditioned beliefs and their exposure to people around them sets their money blueprint. You have heard it said that people's net worth is on par with those they live around and hang out with. Their money blueprints are being set by their surroundings.

....

Taking control of your money blueprint is the key to making more money.

....

There are three simple steps to quickly taking control of your money blueprint:
- Know you have one and determine where it is set.
- Reset it in believable steps.
- When you reset it, write it down as an "I am" statement.

Here's an example: ask yourself how much money you are used to making in a month. Chances are, that is where your blueprint is currently set. Reset that monthly amount at a higher, but believable amount and write it down.

If you are used to making $5,000 per month and you reset your money blueprint at $1 million per month, chances are your conscious mind will not allow that message to penetrate the subconscious. It is simply too unbelievable. You may say, "I am making $1 million per month," but your conscious thinking takes over with too much negativity on that statement.

This is the reason lots of negative people don't believe in affirmations or "I am" statements. They don't realize they simply live their most dominant statements. Remember, your subconscious does not know the difference between what is real and imagined, but in this example, the subconscious may never receive the $1 million message. The conscious goes into overload with doubt and disbelief on that message. It also creates a new statement that is counter to making $1 million per month. That new statement can be something like, "That's ridiculous. You will never make $1 million per month." The sad thing is, you don't even realize it has happened until the damage is done.

No need to worry; you simply set the amount too high. If you are used to making $5,000 per month and you reset your money blueprint at $20,000 per month, chances are your conscious thinking will not rebel on you. It may not totally believe it, and it may not know how you are going to get there, but it won't rebel. Your subconscious will receive the message and begin the manifestation process.

After doing this myself and working with thousands of people in training events and personal coaching, I have found you can usually reset your money blueprint at three to four times what you are currently making and your subconscious will get the message. In my own life I have reset my monthly income blueprint four times, and I currently make ten times what I did when I started. It works. Always have a monthly income amount written as one of your "I am" statements along with other financial goals of your choosing.

Remember, money is a delicate subject. Your subconscious is very sensitive to any messaging it receives around money. To protect your "I am" statements that have anything to do with money or abundance, you want to adjust your daily language.

Try making these changes:

I need money to pay the bills, replaced with, **The bills are being paid.**

How will I pay the mortgage? replaced with, **I sure enjoy my new home.**

How can I make more money? replaced with, **I'm helping people and adding value.**

We need more funds, replaced with, **The funds are flowing in.**

How do I get out of debt? replaced with, **My debts are being paid off.**

We sure need a new car, replaced with, **I love the smell of my new leather seats.**

I was not meant for wealth, replaced with, **I enjoy what my wealth allows me to do.**

I will never afford that, replaced with, **It's nice having the things I want.**

I have to make sacrifices, replaced with, **I have the opportunity.**

I suggest you never say the words, "I can't afford it." Wipe that sentence out of your vocabulary. Replace that with, "I choose not to spend my money on that at this time." This is a huge difference, especially to your subconscious where all things are manifested.

I've already mentioned this next point, but I want to say it again: avoid using the word "sacrifice." Sacrifice means I have to do things so I can get things. With this mindset you are sending out to get. Replace it with the word "opportunity." Opportunity means I get to do things, so I can have things happen for myself and others. With this mindset, you are sending out to give.

One final thought, please remember this: nobody owes you anything. The universe and the people in it owe you nothing. You owe it to yourself to give the universe, and the people in it, everything. Remember, you are sending out to give, which means you act as if you already have. Find out who you are and then give yourself away. Think in terms of abundance and prosperity. Find ways to associate things with abundance and prosperity.

This past winter I was sitting in my hot tub at our cabin in Island Park, Idaho. It was about 6:45 a.m., quiet and very peaceful. At the time, about five feet of snow covered the ground surrounding the cabin. Looking above, I saw about three feet of snow on the roof and it was drifting over the edges. Medium-size snowflakes were falling lightly to the ground—millions of them. In a state of meditation I took several moments to clear my mind and think of nothing but the snowflakes and the peaceful feeling of that snowy morning. After a while, I began to imagine the snowflakes as money—cash money flowing into my life. I then shifted to think on those snowflakes as blessings—of good health, strong relationships, amazing people, fond memories, and good will in the world. And finally, the thought that I am so richly blessed and have so much to be grateful for.

CHAPTER 16

Tenacious Focus

We live in a world where 87 percent of everything we are exposed to is negative. Most people end their day by watching the news before bed, and start their day by listening to the news on the way to work. And then, they browse social media throughout the day and get distracted by lots of negative information. It's not just news channels either. It's everyday drama from people we might or might not know.

At the end of the day this represents distractions that pull us away from our productivity. Yes, we live in a hyper-information world and that is beneficial to us in so many ways. We also live in a hyper-distraction world, and it takes us out of focus on the things we need to be doing.

Even when you are focused on your work, your family, and other productive activities, you get distracted by negativity. You need to find ways to process all this and stay in control of your business and your life.

How do you process and handle negativity when you are faced with:

- Unexpected business situations
- Unexpected life events

- Negative people in your tribe
- Business and economic shifts
- Criticism
- Undermining
- Complaints
- Political rants

The list goes on and on.

I have found the key to circumventing all of this comes down to one thing: tenacious focus on productivity and positivity.

Personally, I struggle with staying focused. I'm a fly-by-the-seat-of-my-pants kind of guy. I enjoy my freedom, I like to be entertained, and I'm somewhat of an adrenaline junkie. I also have a tendency to be emotional. I am a passionate person so I have to bridle my emotional response to things I don't like. Those personality traits pose challenges to staying focused.

Here's what I have found: when I don't stay focused on productivity, then all the negative stimuli quickly takes over my thoughts and emotions. As a result, I've had to find ways to stay focused. I have two saving graces that bail me out on a daily basis: reading and writing. If I didn't have those two things as a focus and practice, I don't know where I would be.

To give you an example of this, my company was working on a major new technology. It was going to completely transform the way we do business. Like all technology-based companies, we need to evolve at a rapid pace and reinvent how we do business. This new technology created new products, new onboarding processes, and even shifted how we branded ourselves. This was a challenging time, to say the least, and we had to manage a lot of unexpected setbacks. We also had to orchestrate several beta launches that led up to a major product launch.

In the midst of all this, we determined that I needed to get this book written and released with a tight deadline. And I needed to prepare for the annual convention of one of my companies. As I mentioned, I enjoy writing so I don't use ghostwriters when I publish my books. I actually write every word. Thank goodness I have excellent editors and designers who make everything look good.

Let me tell you what happened. When I got into the mode of writing this book, I got dialed in or tenaciously focused on everything else. This book is about relationship marketing and my business is about relationship marketing. The tenacious focus on these words, the examples, the lessons, and the stories kept me focused on our business needs as well. In other words, I became better at managing our company needs as I was writing this book.

Here is what is really interesting. The things that normally distract me, like social media drama, complaints, criticisms, uneducated opinions, and everyday challenges, kind of rolled right off my shoulders. I was too focused and too busy to give those things any of my attention.

I'm sure you have heard it said, "If you want to get anything done, find the busiest person you know and ask them to help you get it done." There is a lot of truth to this and I just explained why. Karma works in favor of those who are focused on productivity. Why? Because you are sending out productivity (cause) so you generate productive accomplishment (effect).

AN EAGLE IS TENACIOUSLY FOCUSED

There is a speech I give where I talk about the attributes of an eagle. When I prepared this speech, I wanted to use rhythm and repetition to get people to remember the attributes, so I wrote and performed a rap song. I know that sounds crazy, but I love to rap, so that is what I did.

When you write a rap song, it's ideal to come up with the chorus—or the hook—first. The chorus is the part of the song that everyone seems to know the words to because it is used several times throughout the song. I wrote the chorus and then I wrote three verses. I taught my audiences the chorus and had them rap it while I belted out the three verses. The eagle attributes I wanted them to remember was the chorus. Those words were displayed in four bullet points on the screen

Here is the chorus (the attributes of an eagle)
- Eagles soar, they always **focus** on their goal
- Fly or die, it's how they live and how they roll
- From the nest they jump out to make it happen
- Spread their wings and fly while the chickens flappin'

I put those bullet points up on the screen, played the music, rapped those words with the music so they could hear it, and then I had them stand and try it. Then I gave my speech. The four bullet points were the outline to the speech. It went something like this:

- **Eagles soar, they always focus on their goal:**

Eagles are majestic. They can hold you spellbound as you watch them effortlessly soar in the sky. They have amazing eyesight and they stay incredibly focused.

An eagle can be flying several thousand feet in the air, focus in on a fish that is several feet under the water, go into an air dive that can reach over 100 miles per hour, reach her talons out and use her wings to slow down the dive. She will reach those talons several feet under the water and grab that fish. The whole time the eagle is doing this, she never takes her eyes off that fish.

We too can take on this attribute. To be like the eagle, we need to stay laser focused on our goals, never take our eye off the mark, and not allow distractions to keep us from what we are working toward.

- **Fly or die, it's how they live and how they roll:**

An eagle instinctively knows that if she does not teach her eaglets how to fly, they will die. A mother eagle is very caring, loving and nurturing to her eaglets for about the first seven weeks of their life. Around the seventh week, the mother eagle will do things to make the family nest uncomfortable. She will find thorns and sharp branches and put them in the center of the nest. This causes the eaglets to move toward the edge of the nest. These nests are typically built high above the ground, in a tree or along cliff edges.

As the eaglet gets to the edge, the mother eagle will nudge him out of the nest for his first flight. Usually the eaglet wildly flaps his wings as he lunges towards the ground. The mother eagle will swoop down under the falling eaglet, catch him on her back, and majestically fly him back to the nest for another try. They do this until the eaglet learns how to fly like its mother.

We too can take on this attribute. We need to know that we are either flying or we are dying, which means we are either producing or we are stagnant. If we are not being productive in our business, with our families, and with all aspects of our lives, we become stale. We were not meant to sit around and do nothing. We were meant to do things, to make a difference, to be an inspiration, to build, to enjoy. This is what flying is all about.

- **From the nest they jump out to make it happen**

Eagles are the best hunters in the prey. An eagle will hit its mark 50 percent of the time. The second best hunter in the prey is a wolf. A wolf will hit its prey around 12 percent of the time. This shows you just how successful an eagle is. The interesting thing about this statistic is that if the eagle hits its prey 50 percent of the time, that means she misses 50 percent of the time. Think about that. One time out of two, the eagle misses.

I want you to think about something. What happens when an eagle comes out of the sky and reaches her talons down to grab a running rabbit who finds a hole at the last second and crawls under the ground to safety? Can you imagine that eagle flying back to its perch and starting to whine and complain about missing her mark? Come on now, use your imagination. The eagle gets back to her perch and says, "It's not fair. That hole was not supposed to be there. That rabbit was lucky. The wind blew me off course and it's not fair. What am I going to do now? Oh no."

Of course that is ridiculous. That eagle gets back to her perch and immediately seeks out her next target. She doesn't think about the miss for one second; she is already focused on where to go next. That eagle knows the law of averages. She knows that one out of two times she will hit the mark, so she just gets back and focuses on the next hit.

If we want to take on the attributes of the eagle we need to act the same way. There is no room or time for whining and complaining. We need to learn what our law of averages are and keep on aiming for the goal. Keep moving forward. If you are in sales, then network like crazy and keep your pipeline full. You need to have so many people to talk to that it doesn't matter when someone says yes or no to you. You just keep working with people every day. Some will, some won't, so what, move on to the next (SW, SW, SW, NEXT).

- **Spread their wings and fly while the chickens flappin'**

The highest-flying bird in the world is the eagle. An eagle can fly as high as 20,000 feet in the air. The lowest-flying bird in the world is a chicken. A chicken can only get a couple of feet off the ground.

Eagles don't use a tremendous amount of their own energy. An eagle will leave her perch and gracefully use her wings to gain some momentum in flight. The eagle will find natural updrafts of wind and fly in a circular motion and allow the updraft to carry them upward. When they catch these drafts they actually will rest their wings and allow the wind to push them up. That is how they are able to reach the height of 20,000 feet.

The biggest enemy to the eagle is the crow. A crow will actually chase an eagle. The crow makes an obnoxious sound as it flies. It will chase the eagle and can get as high as about 7,000 feet. The crow expends its own energy while the eagle flies smarter. The eagle will simply rise above the noise and get away from the distractions of the crow. The chicken will viciously flap its wings to try and take flight. They flap so hard that they lose feathers in the process. They only get a couple of feet off the ground.

We too can take on the attribute of the eagle. We can spread our wings and fly above the noise of negativity and mediocrity. We can work smart by giving to the world instead of trying to get from the world. We don't want to be like the chicken and try to force things to happen. We can be like the eagle and allow things to happen by being smart with our actions and staying in a positive vibrational state of energy.

- Eagles soar, we always focus on our goal
- Fly or die, it's how we live and how we roll
- From the nest we jump out to make it happen
- Spread our wings and fly while the chickens flappin'

I suggest we all move forward and take on the attributes of the eagle. Tenacious focus is the key to overcoming the things that try to hold us down. It will keep us in a productive state and on the right side of karma. To embrace the true power of human connection we need to be like the eagle: stay focused on our goals, stay in a constant state of productivity, play the law of averages in everything we do, and rise above the noise and clutter we face in our lives.

CHAPTER 17

An Attitude of Gratitude

We have discussed a powerful concept throughout this book that says what you appreciate, appreciates. This simply means the things you share gratitude and appreciation for will grow. Appreciate your relationships and they will get stronger. Appreciate your money and it will appreciate, or grow. Appreciate life and life will appreciate you back. It's a simple but fundamental law.

If you show gratitude to other people then other people will show gratitude to you. This is certainly true but it's not the most powerful part of what happens. When you show gratitude to other people, then you will feel gratitude from yourself.

I know this is a new thought for some, but you need to allow it to sink in. Your self worth and self-esteem appreciates, or gets bigger, when you appreciate other people. As you send out gratitude, others will send back gratitude, but what happens within is what is transformational.

The power of human connection includes not only how you connect with others, but also how you connect with yourself. There is the "you" that is and there is the "you" that is meant to be. When those two things come together, then the greatest of human connection takes place. A person who is connected to self is a person who can make the greatest connections with others. The greatest attribute and activity for connection with self and others is gratitude.

Several years ago, we started issuing gratitude challenges to people within our company. We asked them to use our card-sending system to send daily gratitude to others. We did seven-day challenges and 30-day challenges.

Our purpose was two-fold. First, we wanted more people to feel appreciated. Second, we wanted the sender to see if this challenge would have a positive impact on them.

After doing this challenge myself and hearing so many inspirational stories, I wrote a song to describe the transformational process that I and others experienced. The song talks about how someone first received a card of gratitude. He explains the profound effect that had on him. The person who sent him the card invited him to join a gratitude challenge where he could send cards to others like the one he had received. He took that challenge and the song tells us what happened.

Allow me to share the lyrics of this song:

Gratitude Rap Song (Lyrics)

First Verse
*I got an old friend who made me feel good
hadn't talked in a while but I understood
when he sent me a card, said he's grateful for me
and he said I helped him out to be the best that he could be.
Words couldn't explain the power of his expression
how they lifted me up and brought me out of depression.*

I didn't even know that I influenced his action,
that I gave him hope and a sense of satisfaction.
It's amazing what some words of gratitude will do
it's like they saved me and gave me a chance to renew
so I called and thanked him for making my day and greater gift
was found and this is what he had to say.

Chorus

So stand, stand up and cheer for people far and near were sending love not fear with gratitude

and for you to find your way I challenge you today reach out with what you say with gratitude

Verse 2

And I was so inspired with appreciation

I took him up on his challenge to pass the sensation I started thinking of people once a day for 30 days that I could say thank you for how they steered my way.

I thought of Aunt Sally, my old friend Sam, my eighth grade teacher, they're part of who I am,

I started sending them cards so in my heart they could see the difference that they made to me.

So by day nine or 10 I noticed a shift and how the sender of the cards was just getting this lift.

Then my attitude got better the good was everywhere the gratitude challenge is everything that I'mma share.

Chorus

So stand, stand up and cheer for people far and near were sending love not fear with gratitude and for you to find your way I challenge you today reach out with what you say with gratitude.

We produced this song into a music video and you can view it at www.kodybateman.com. Click on music videos and select the Gratitude Music Video.

Over the years, we have collected inspiring stories from people who consistently sent cards of gratitude. I'd like to share a few with you.

The first story comes from Kathy Paauw, a dear friend and relationship marketing expert who has helped thousands of people share gratitude. This story shows you the powerful effects of gratitude on the person who is sharing it.

It was September 2005, and our only child was headed off to attend college in Minnesota. The 1,700-mile distance between Seattle, Washington, and Northfield, Minnesota, was really hard on both my husband and me.

That same week, I received news that my mother was ready to do an intervention with my brother, who had struggled with substance abuse for many years. (For those who are not familiar with this, an intervention is a professionally directed face-to-face meeting of family members, friends and employers with the person addicted to alcohol or drugs. The purpose is to get the individual to seek professional help with their addiction.) Since my mother was his enabler, I had prayed for her to be open to getting this professional help for at least 15 years, but I was not happy with the timing of her decision to do it.

The intervention meeting did not go well. After it ended, my mother had an accident and was taken to the hospital ER with a broken nose and some cuts requiring stitches. My brother took off to pay a visit to some drug dealers for his cocaine fix. With all that going on, I sank into a deep depression.

A friend called to check on me, and during our conversation she asked if I would commit to a daily ritual she'd recently started doing that was helping her rise above her own deep depression after her daughter's suicide. My friend asked me to begin each day by sending a card of gratitude to someone. She showed me a system I could access online that would send real greeting cards that I selected or built from my computer. While we were still on the phone, she helped me create and send a card from my laptop.

The first card I sent was to my husband, who was also feeling very down with our daughter being so far away and everything else that was going on. When I pressed the "send" button, my friend told me the service would print, stuff, address, stamp, and take it to the post office for me the next day. The US Postal Service would deliver this first-class mail to the address on the envelope within a few days.

Although I was not feeling very grateful at the time, I reluctantly agreed to my friend's request, and I promised her I'd send out a card of gratitude each morning for the next seven days.

The next morning, I dragged myself out of bed and went downstairs to my office, where I slumped into my chair and asked, "What am I grateful for?" Eventually I thought of someone and I created a card, using the system my friend had just introduced me to.

It was really hard at first, but each day it got easier to think of who I was grateful for. Below is one of the seven cards I sent.

Dear Marilyn,

The other day I was feeling down, and you lifted me up with your smile and an encouraging word. Although you may not have known it, my brief conversation with you made the rest of my day so much better. I appreciate your support and encouragement.

You continue to inspire those around you, including me. Thanks for the many big and small ways you make this world a better place, just by showing up and being you.

With love and gratitude,
Kathy

Make Life... Your Work of Art

Sure enough, a few days later our postal carrier delivered the card I had sent to my husband. When he opened it, a big smile came across his face; that made me smile, too.

To my surprise, by the end of the seven days my depression had lifted. I also started getting amazing responses from those who had received my cards. I discovered that sending cards that expressed gratitude and kindness had multiple positive impacts: It made me (the sender) feel good, it made the recipient feel good, and it created a positive ripple effect as both of us spread kindness to others throughout the day.

I loved this relationship-building tool so much that I decided to continue using it daily and sharing it with others. That was more than 12 years ago and I continue to send daily cards of gratitude from my SendOutCards relationship-building system.

In case you're wondering what happened with my brother—within a week of the intervention meeting, he agreed to get help. Nine months later, he graduated from the treatment program we'd arranged for him, and he stayed clean and so-ber for the remainder of his life. Unfortunately, my brother passed away from a fatal heart attack at the age of 56.

There is no better time than now to tell others how much we love and appreciate them, and to find ways to unite our divided and hurting world.

The next story comes from Richard de Groot, who shows us the power of gratitude within the "good ole boys club."

I have done three gratitude challenges over the last few years and all of them were 30-day challenges. Two stories stand out for me. Both of them were gratitude cards I sent to people who had been my friends for more than 30 years.

I simply told them I loved them and that I appreciated their friendship very much, and said I sent this card to actually let them know this personally because us guys never do this, we just grunt.

The first friend took four days to call me after he got the card, as he did not know what to say or how to respond. When he did call, he was in tears because the card really touched his heart.

The second friend did not call me, so after a week I called him instead, asking if he had received the card. He said, "Yes, but why did you send the card?" I responded, "I just felt like I needed to say this to you." After a few seconds of silence, he said he did not ring me back because he did not know what to say or how to respond to my card. While saying this, he broke down in tears and shared that nobody had ever told him that he was appreciated, they just grunted.

I love this story because it reminds us that men, in particular, often have a hard time expressing their gratitude to other men. It's kind of a macho thing to have a cool handshake and, like Richard says, just grunt. But you can see how important and powerful the expression is. It creates connection and allows people to know that they matter. I guess you could say it changes grunts to tears.

This next story comes from Scott and Sandee Giller. This story shows the power of gratitude when you express it to people you don't yet know.

We have done a few of the Gratitude Challenges, and one of the things we have really made a point to do is thanking wait staff that we have had along the way.

We have a number of gratitude stories, but these two are our favorites.

1. I used to go to the same Dunkin' Donuts every morning on the way to work. The lady in the window was amazing; she would write smiley faces and cute notes on my cup. She even noticed when I wasn't there for a day or two. I asked to take her photo and I sent her a card and brownies thanking her for starting my day off with a smile (I sent it just before leaving for vacation). When I got back, and got up to the drive-through window, she had tears running down her face. She said that she had moved here from Brazil and didn't

know anyone, so she took photos of the card and texted them to her family.

A few weeks later, when I was there, she had tears again. The regional bigwigs had come through and saw the card I sent her on the bulletin board. They interviewed her and wrote an article about her and her awesome customer service that was in the international Dunkin' Donuts newsletter that went to every Dunkin' Donuts in the world.

2. Just after returning from a cruise, Scott and I stopped at the Bubba Gump restaurant on Santa Monica Pier. We had a really great waitress (Hilary). We started chatting with her and we asked her if she liked brownies. Of course she said yes. We took her photo and asked her for her address. She told one of the other waiters (Raymon), who happened to be walking by, that she was getting free brownies. He asked what he had to do to earn free brownies. We told him he had to tell us something funny. He actually ended up being funnier than the comedian on the cruise we had just been on. We asked him for his address and took his photo as well. On the way out of the restaurant we took a business card with the manager's name on it. We sent a card to each of the wait staff to their homes and a big card to the manager of Bubba Gump. In the card we told him what amazing staff these two were and how he should be honored to have them as part of his team.

Fast forward nine months to September 2015. Scott and I rented a van to pick up several of our friends and business associates from the airport. We were traveling together to attend a large relationship marketing event. We brought them to the same Bubba Gump on Santa Monica Pier. We asked if either Hilary or Raymon were there. Only Raymon was. We asked if we could say hello to him. When he came over to our table, he held his heart and said, "I am not going to lie, I do not remember your names, but I will NEVER forget what you did for me." We then introduced him to everyone. He then told our group that not only did we send him the most amazing brownies and card, but we sent a card to his manager. He said that his manager set the card up on the bulletin board and used it as part of the trainings for the staff. Raymon said we totally changed his life.

This next story, shared by Patty Doskis, shows us the power of gratitude when you share it in a long-distance relationship with someone you have never met:

In 2013, I did a 30-Day Gratitude Challenge. I sent a few cards to my colleague and friend Ann, who was battling cancer. We worked for the same company but we had never met face to face. We became friends over the phone and through email exchanges; I live in New Jersey, and she lived in Albuquerque. I sent her cards of encouragement and gratitude to uplift her during rough days of chemo and radiation. Upon receiving my cards, she was so touched that she wanted to call me before heading to the hospital for her chemo treatment. She called and her husband put the call on speaker. We cried and she told me how much the cards meant to her and she could not thank me enough. Ann lost her battle a month later. Though I was sad to lose her, our final conversation is what I hold dear to my heart. It was about love, gratitude, and peace, and I'm thankful for that moment I had with her.

The following story comes from Jessy Fraser of Phoenix, Arizona. This story demonstrates the power of gratitude within the most important kind of relationship of all, the family:

My parents' anniversary was coming up and I decided to create a unique card for them. My parents met in high school and married when they were just 20 and 21. I am the oldest of four. I have a brother and two sisters. All my siblings are married and have children of their own. The youngest sister, age 21, has a one year old, and the others both have two children. My mom is a Facebook addict so she's always posting photos of everything! She had posted old pictures of when she first started dating my father. I took those pictures and used my card-sending system to copy and paste them on the front of a card. I also included pictures of just them during holidays from the past to the present. On the inside of the card I included photos of all my siblings, their spouses and their children. I also included photos of pets and a special quote.

I sent the card not expecting what happened next. I got a call a few days later from my father; he could hardly speak. My dad is such a macho man. Being Latino, he hardly ever shows his softer side. He was sobbing on the phone thanking me for the card and for making him see what he had created. He told me that he just works and provides for us.

He said he had never stopped to see life happening, to see what he had worked hard all his life for. He said that all the pictures in the card would not have happened if it wasn't for his love for my mother. He thanked me for allowing him to see the bigger picture. This feeling is something my father and I won't ever forget.

I hope you are starting to see a trend here. These simple expressions of gratitude are transformational, not only to the receiver but also to the sender. We are not talking about theories here. We are talking about real life stories that show you the power of human connection via gratitude.

As you can probably see, I could do an entire book of gratitude stories like these. We have thousands of them, as people have done these gratitude challenges all over the world. I only shared a handful of stories, but they show how gratitude helped clear depression, how it bonded friendships of brotherly love, how it created a lasting connection among total strangers, how it cemented an eternal friendship between two people who had never met in person, and it powerfully displayed the power of a husband who loved his wife and created a loving family who deeply appreciates their parents.

This is human connection at its very best. It creates the energy that builds those things that truly matter. What you appreciate, appreciates. It gets bigger, better, more powerful, more loving, kind, generous, and giving. With a simple attitude of gratitude, we can and we are transforming the world to a higher state of living.

You can choose to focus on the trends of social media and comment and complain on everything under the sun if you want to. You can choose to buy into the media chaos and mis-representation if you want to. You can choose to find drama and get caught up in tearing others down if you want to. But I will choose gratitude every time. It's simply a better way to live.

CHAPTER 18

Bringing the World Together with the Power of Human Connection

W e have learned that genuine human connection is the key to successful relationship marketing. It is also the key to success in life. Relationships are everything. This includes relationship with self and with others, including those we do business with.

We have also learned that karma generates the power of human connection at every level. The first 12 chapters of this book focused on the power of human connection in business. We learned what true relationship marketing means and how to do it. Within those chapters we also learned about human connection with those in our personal life including friends, neighbors and family members. Through the process, hopefully you witnessed that the line between a business associate and a friend becomes blurry. At the end of the day, everything we do is about creating human connection. What we do for a living is merely a way for us to participate in the world and interact with others.

The last five chapters have specifically focused on your individual personal development. They have covered how you can make connection with you, with your potential—with the "you" that is meant to be.

In this concluding chapter, I want to discuss the power of human connection at a much bigger level. It's the connection of the human race. I believe you can take the principles of this book and apply them to bringing the human race together. When I say the "power" of human connection, I believe it. I believe we do have the power within us to come together.

It all starts with finding out who you are so you can give yourself away to others. To do this I ask you to explore the defining moments you have had in your life. I've had many defining moments in mine. Most of them have evolved into a common theme that defines who I am as a person.

I don't believe I am unique to this experience. In fact, I believe we all have a common theme that our defining moments are based on. It's important to explore your life experiences and discover what that common theme is for you. It is there that we find our own uniqueness, the genius we have to offer the world.

When we find it, we must stand for it, live it, be it. At the end of the day, I have to **do me,** and you have to **do you.** Those who are true to themselves have an easier time accepting others who are being true to themselves. This is where peace, harmony, productivity, and potential are realized.

Allow me to share the journey that led me to the common theme of my life. Perhaps this will help you to explore your own.

I think my most significant defining moment took place when I, a young white man, lived in an all-black neighborhood in Baltimore Maryland. Many of you have heard my stories of McCabe Avenue. I lived there in 1984 when I was only 20 years old. In the first few days of walking down McCabe, I was not accepted by many because I am white. For the first time in my 20 years of living, I truly felt what it was like to be the minority.

My first day in that neighborhood I met Tony Watson, a 17-year-old black kid who accepted me, and we became close friends. He taught me how to rap. We had incredible times on those streets and I became accepted as part of the neighborhood. I was amazed by what I learned from a group of people who lived where what many would call the wrong side of the tracks—the ghetto. It was there that I learned even though we came from different backgrounds and were born into different races, we had the same desires to love, be loved, pursue dreams, and make a difference in the world.

I learned on McCabe Avenue that this game called humanity is really quite simple. It's our societies and what we learn that makes it complicated. Hatred, separation, prejudice, and even racism, are learned evils. Often those emotions and beliefs run very deep.

When I was on McCabe, it had only been 19 years since the height of the civil rights movement. And though racial tensions were still felt, it seemed as if our society had made lots of progress. Today we have added another 33-plus years to our history, and unfortunately, it seems as if we have digressed in the all-important category of getting along as human beings.

I will never claim to understand where everyone is coming from or what all the answers might be to bring us back together again. But I do know this. In 1984, a 20-year-old white young man and a 17-year-old black young man were the closest of friends living in an all-black neighborhood. We danced in the streets and busted out rhymes. We were friends with everyone. This was my defining moment and every defining moment since has been related to me being a solution to bringing people together.

I learned an important message back then, and that message has become the theme of my life. I can sum it up with these words: our world is blessed with numerous ethnic groups of people. But there is only one race; it's called the human race. We are all brothers and sisters in this game called life and we can learn so much from each other. I believe that becoming united as a people is the true test we must pass as human beings. To do this we must believe in a world that is rich in ethnic diversity and united in our resolve to be one group, one family, and one race.

Being united as a people must be the priority. And though that may not be the case for many, it will be the case for me and everything I stand for. We are united as a people, and united we send out who we are to the world.

Another thing that impressed me on those streets was that people were real. They were true to who they were and not afraid to express their uniqueness. I loved that about the streets of Baltimore. In that attitude I witnessed amazing talent. The kids on those streets were expressive through music, artwork, poetry, and words; they were masters of words with the ability to communicate with passion. That's why to this day I have a love for hip-hop and rap. It brings out the expressive nature of a rich culture. So many amazing stories of lives lived are expressed in brilliant poetry delivered through rhythm and rhyme.

I understand that I share this passion and interest with perhaps a small segment of the world's population. Many people are not into hip-hop and rap and have never had the experiences I've had. Those people have had their own life experiences, their own defining moments, and their own common themes that drive them. And isn't that the way it is supposed to be? It's not in sameness that we experience what life has to offer us. It is in differences. Diversity is the greatest blessing of the universe.

If I can get tuned into the common theme of my life and just do me, then I know my contribution will make a difference. And how can I do that if I don't respect or celebrate the common theme of others? Your contribution blesses my life as mine blesses yours. This is not complicated. It's a simple formula that blesses you with a life of passion, peace, and joy.

So the defining moments of my life have evolved into a service that can help people become united. Together we can offer this service to the world. We can also offer an opportunity along with that service that gives people something they can build for themselves and their families.

In the climate of today's world, we need to realize how significant this is. We have a service that can help people come together again. We also have an opportunity where people can actively build something of financial and spiritual significance. In a world where people are quick to judge others and seek to tear things down, we can provide the antidote. When you are actively engaged in producing or building something, it's not even possible for you to loot or tear things down.

In the classic book *Atlas Shrugged* written by Ayn Rand in 1957, we are taken on a brilliant fictional story where heads of big industry (known as producers in the book) are struggling to keep their businesses operational. Their opposition comes from regulators (known as looters in the book) who continue to gain power and stifle the growth of the producers. As the storyline continues, the producers start disappearing and it's a great mystery as to where they have gone. Later, a character by the name of John Galt shows up and offers the producers a new society where production can thrive once again. Though some view this book as politically controversial, it points out a simple fact: in our world we have people who build things (producers) and people who tear things down (looters). We are also constantly seeking a solution to a stronger economy and a better society in which to live. In the book, that solution comes in the name of John Galt.

What I propose to you today is we have found John Galt. We have created the representation of his character in the opportunity that each of us holds in our hands. We do have a better way, a way that turns people into producers. We have a system backed by a philosophy that can bring people back together again. So take this opportunity and **do you** and celebrate other people when they do the same. The world will be much better for it.

To summarize the significance of being true to who you are, I have written what I call the *Do You Manifesto*. I hope its words will resonate with you and inspire you to bless us with your genius.

Do You Manifesto
Worry about what others think and you
End up confused with little direction
Slow to manifest your dreams—frustrated
You lose hope and only find solace in watching
Other stories of dreams lived

Then you see some who are not afraid to be who they are
Yet others who still might be
and they miss the message that comes from the uniqueness
around them

None of this madness stops until you become true to you

When you do you, you begin to celebrate others who do the same
And it's only then that your life moves upward
Momentum is gained
Persistence prevails
Respect is shown to others regardless of difference

We come to know that families—mine and yours—
Are most important
We all have are dreams and seek happiness
But sometimes our social devices steal our focus
We get caught up in others' chatter
Quickly lose sight that all lives matter
And it only makes the world sadder

Conflict only breeds more conflict
Love and peace bring to pass the civil rights of all
There is only one race
With every human leaving their own unique thumbprint

We can celebrate our differences when we focus
On how we are all the same
To love and be loved is how the human race evolves as one
The process begins and ends with you. Just do you and win
Be the best version of you and you become a producer in society
A builder
A doer
A creator
When you actively build something
Your mind cannot process tearing something down.

The world and the people in it owe you nothing
But you owe it to yourself to give the world
and the people in it everything

Find out who you are and give yourself away
This is how we all stand together as one

In chapter 11, I talked about creating your personal brand. Go back and study that. It shares how to write down "I am" statements and come up with a personal branding statement that represents your purpose. This is the statement that represents who you are; it's what you have to offer the world.

Mine says, "I bring the human race together." As you can see, this is a big part of me. There is no way I can finish this book without writing about it.

Once again, explore the defining moments of your life, write down your "I am" statements and create your own personal branding statement. Do you. Find out who you are and give yourself away to the world. By doing that, you will offer the best version of you to the world. You will realize the power of human connection by sending your best to others and you will create human connection that will transform every area of your life.

True connection with self allows you to connect with others at a much deeper level. Deeper connection with others will nourish self to reach its highest potential.

I wish you the best of success on your journey to give the best version of you away to the world. I'm counting on you. We need you. Make it happen.

HOW RELATIONSHIP MARKETING IS
TRANSFORMING THE WAY PEOPLE SUCCEED

Riches in the Niches

Sending a real greeting card in the mail is probably one of the greatest traditions we have in the world—an opportunity for us to share kindness, thank someone, or reach out to create a genuine human connection. When you send out to give, you also trigger yourself into gratitude, and when you stay in gratitude, gratitude will also find you. Throughout this book I talked about creating genuine human connection and building relationships as a way to grow your business. It's not for the purpose of a return on investment, or gaining more business, or building your brand. Send because you want to celebrate the people you're sending the card to. Focus on that, because that's what the world needs. You'll find that your business will grow and your relationships will multiply as you thank through the process of building your business and your personal relationships.

Throughout the book I shared examples of how people thank their customers through the process. I want to share a few more examples from guests on my *Relationship Marketing Weekly* show who shared examples of how appreciating their customers increased their businesses exponentially. A lot of people don't realize how powerful appreciation can be. They may think, "Well, if I'm going to send a thank you card, I will send it when the business is done or when I get the business." And less than 3 percent of people in the business world today send a thank you card at all, even though that is the most impactful marketing touch you can send to a prospect or to a client to inspire referral business.

Over the past year, I've interviewed people from 50 different business niches who have transformed their businesses using relationship marketing—by appreciating their customers and prospects and thanking them through the process with cards and gifts. I mentioned several of these stories throughout the book, and I reference those for you first. Following are many more examples from guests on my *Relationship Marketing Weekly* show. All together, these examples touch many different business niches. If they don't touch your particular niche, I'd love to hear how you have used appreciation to build your own business. You can share your story with me at info@kodybateman.com.

REAL ESTATE
Gayle Zientek (page 36)

INSURANCE
Hugh Thompson (page 40)

TREE SERVICE
Dave Potter (page 57)

COMMERCIAL AND RESIDENTIAL CONSTRUCTION
Heba Malki (page 64)

COLLISION REPAIR
Andre Perdue (page 67)

CUSTOM HOMEBUILDER
Paul Rising (page 69)

MASTER NETWORKER
Jordan Adler (page 76)

NETWORKING, FOUNDER OF BNI
Ivan Misner (page 79)

AUTO REPAIR
Tom Lambert (page 87)

AUTO SALES
Chris Kendall (page 150)

CORPORATE RETENTION AND APPRECIATION
Gregg Bryars (page 160)

LAW ENFORCEMENT RECRUITMENT AND APPRECIATION
Dean Gialamas (page 162)

INTERNET MARKETER
Tanya Aliza

Tanya Aliza is a rockstar internet marketer, and a masterful teacher in the internet marketing world. She's run a very successful, seven-figure business online since 2010, teaching entrepreneurs how to use tools, automation, and build sales funnels. She is also a coach and has an online training business. But to promote her business, she actually uses an offline system. When she was a guest on my *Relationship Marketing Weekly* show, I asked Tanya how an internet marketer can get personal with an online customer.

It doesn't matter if you're working online with your customers. It's about building a connection. With my team, our mantra is, "The customer is always taken care of." In my business, we have the most skeptical people in the world. People are still scared today to use their credit card online to buy something. So when we make a sale, that's not the end of the road for us—it's more like the beginning. We have a 30-day refund policy, so it's really, really important to us to get the value into our customers' hands and alleviate the skepticism. But it's also really important to have high touch in such a low-touch world.

A lot of people in internet marketing think they can just sell stuff and then go hit the beach. But you also have to take great care of your customers. We've built our reputation and repeat client base because we take care of them with high touches. We phone them personally every time they make an order, and we also send them a greeting card in the mail. We have Facebook groups for all of our customers. When they get the card in the mail, they're so excited and they post a picture in the group saying, "I just received my Tanya Aliza greeting card! Thank you so much. This is awesome."

With that, we solidify the sale, but we also solidify the relationship for life. I've turned some of the people who have come into my world and spent $7 or $297 into clients who have spent all the way up to $25,000 with me. It's really,

really huge in a low-touch online world to really take it off-line and make them feel special and golden in your world, to make yourself stand out as the person on the other side of that transaction. My clients love it. No other internet marketer does this. It really separates us from the others. We have less than a 1 percent refund rate per month on our products in an industry where 10 percent is average. I believe our extremely low refund rate has to do with how we treat our customers—we make them feel special. When customers join my annual mastermind, we send them a VIP welcome card and brownies. For my mastermind higher-end clients, we send them a birthday card and a little gift as well.

I also like to network and follow up with people I meet at these events. I was at a networking event six years ago where I collected a bunch of business cards. When I got home, I went through all of the cards and put aside the ones I wanted to stay connected with. With one card, I had taken a selfie with the person, and I sent him a card with our photo on it. He put it up on his refrigerator where he saw it every day. He started doing some webinar training for my community. We started talking on Skype. And he happens to be my husband today. We just celebrated our one-year anniversary a few months ago. He calls it the law of attraction because he put me on his fridge and stared at me every day.

When you're a business owner or an aspiring business owner or entrepreneur, it's not about the money. It's about the relationships first, before the money. If you can remember that and cultivate those relationships, what you put out is what you get in. You will go far in your personal life and also in business.

SALON AND SPA
Darla DiGrandi

Darla DiGrandi started a salon and day spa more than 30 years ago, in her young twenties. She built it into an enterprise with 49 employees, 16,000 clients, and more than five salons, all in the Palm Springs, California, area. She sold items at a premium when the competition was cutting prices. I think it's safe to say Darla does things differently. Even before she had access to a state-of-the-art appreciation card system, Darla was sending cards of appreciation to every customer who came in to her salon.

As a little girl, I had a dream to have the largest, most expensive salon in town. I was the first day spa to open in our area that was not connected to a resort, and I was a big dreamer. I had big visions, but I didn't have any money. I was a young 20-something just out of beauty school, working in a salon. Right away I thought, "I've got to do this. I've got to build these dreams. I can do this." I got started on my own in a two-chair salon and began hiring people and training them. My employees were really young. I taught them how to shake hands, look people in the eye, greet them by their first name, and to say, "We appreciate you and thank you."

As a kid, I remember reading in the *Guinness Book of World Records* about the guy who was the number one salesman because he hand-wrote thank you cards every day to people who came in to his business. We couldn't afford big advertising, but from the very beginning, we implemented appreciation marketing in the form of a thank you card. We sent out little white postcards with a printed label that had a simple message: "Thank you for visiting and we appreciate your business." Every month we'd run reports, and if our clients didn't come in the next month we'd send them a card that said, "Haven't seen you in a while." We always tracked our numbers and the number one most solid source of customers came from word-of-mouth referrals from people who were already coming to us. As our salons grew, we put mail rooms in them with huge printing machines so we could print our cards of gratitude, appreciation, haven't-seen-you, and happy birthday.

Think about it. Why do you go somewhere? You don't go there because of the price. You go there because you're appreciated. So right out of beauty school, my haircuts were $20-something. We were frying hair every day, doing bad haircuts and making people cry at the most expensive price. But they stayed with us because we always sent them a thank you card and thanked them for being a part of our growth and our business. We were booked for weeks in advance. You couldn't get an appointment with us and that was because we knew how to make people feel important and appreciated by constantly thanking them and telling them how much we appreciated them.

When I sold my salons and left the business, I became a salon consultant. People would pay me to come into their salons and teach them how to implement this in their business so they could raise their prices and become a high-end salon.

After I sold my salons I ran into Kody's company and relationship marketing system, and I haven't slept since. There are so many things you can do today that you couldn't do back then! If we'd had this system back then, I could have been doing some just *beyond* things! Back when I started, we always said, "I wish we could put a before and after picture on that card." But you couldn't do that back then. The technology didn't exist.

The number one reason a customer will leave your business is not because of price or service. It's a perceived indifference. They think you don't care about them. Just start showing gratitude. It's so easy now to put a before and after picture on a card. If every spa or salon owner will take a before and after picture, even the ones their clients post to social media, and put it on a card and send it to them, they will change the entire dynamic of what they're creating with that gratitude.

For a brief time, when social media and email were new, we switched to emailing and posting our comments. But this completed removed the personal touch. When you post a message on Facebook, it's gone in an instant. When you send a card that says, "You look beautiful! Thank you for coming to me to get your hair done," it's something they can hang on their wall or display on their desk. It's a keepsake.

Any business, any person, thing, or place that is successful has a large network of people who are fans, supporters, customers, whatever. Where did those people come from? They came from somebody else telling them or inviting them or referring them. Where did *those* people come from? Someone else telling them or inviting them or referring them. They didn't come from a Yellow Pages ad. With appreciation and referral marketing, you can eliminate every other type of marketing on the planet and you will now attract people into your life through them telling other people about you. If you are brave enough to try it, you will instantly see what I mean.

Here's the power of this system just for a hair salon. Imagine you took a picture of a little girl coming in to get her first haircut, and you put her picture inside a card with a nice message. She's going to keep this card and you're going to have her as a client for the rest of her life. She's going to show all of her friends these cards. When a wedding party comes in and you're going to do the whole wedding ceremony, or maybe prom or graduation, put these photos in a big card and send your clients pictures of their experience, of their moment.

Darla grows her business exponentially with appreciation you can touch. She created a tribe of raving fans by showing tangible appreciation with greeting cards. The proof of relationship marketing shows up over and over again in the success of businesses in all niches.

RECRUITING PROFESSIONAL
Bijan Yusufzai

Bijan Yusufzai runs Infinite Talent Group in Sydney, Australia. He is a corporate recruiter who finds technology talent for large corporations, a specialized and highly competitive niche. Using the relationship marketing tools found in SendOutCards, Bijan has cultivated a strong network that can be tapped for top IT talent, and it also keeps him top of mind and ahead of the pack.

I have one story I love to share; I call it my $250,000 card story. For quite a while I had been pursuing a potential client who was a senior project director running an IT project. I knew quite a few other people who worked on the project as well. The challenge was, this project director was very busy, and I knew there were a bunch of other recruiters who also wanted to supply IT talent for this project. Every time I tried to approach her by email or phone, her personal assistant would say, "I'm sorry. She's not available. She's in a meeting. Call another time." And this went on for close to a year.

But I never really gave up. Every few weeks or a couple of months, I would call again and try to see if I could get in touch with her. One time when I called, her personal assistant said, "Sorry. She's actually not in the office. She had to leave because her mom passed away. She's in a different state. She will be back in about two weeks. Try again."

Wow, I felt so bad that she had just lost her mom! But as soon as I hung up the phone, the thought came to me to send her a condolence card. So I went to SendOutCards online and created a card that said, "Sorry for your loss. Hoping that you and your family are doing well. If there's anything I can do to help, please let me know." It was a really simple card. But I sent it off to her and then I forgot about it.

In about two weeks' time, I answered an unexpected call and it was this director. She said, "I just wanted to call you and say thank you for the card. It really touched my heart. When I came back, obviously I was upset with the loss of my mom. There was only one card, and it was sitting on my desk." She expressed her appreciation and then said, "What do you do? How can I help?"

I said, "In the last few months, I've been trying to reach out to you. I've got this amazing consultant who can help you out with the project." I wasn't in her panel of approved vendors, but we set up a time that I could fly out and meet her. Even though she's an incredibly busy person, we ended up sitting and chatting in a café for about two-and-a-half hours. We talked less about work and more about her family, her children, and where she lives. It was an amazing conversation and a connection. When we were finished, she said, "I'm going to call the procurement manager. I want to make sure you are on our panel and we're going to start working together." This interaction translated into $250,000 for that particular project, which is still ongoing. And we still have a very good business relationship.

Making a connection on a personal level is what relationship marketing—and life—is all about. Sometimes we forget that businesses are run by people. Bijan simply acted on a prompting to send a heartfelt sympathy card, and it resulted in what will probably be a lifelong business relationship with someone who is now a connection in his sphere.

ADMISSIONS DIRECTOR, MONTESSORI SCHOOL
Darla Fanta

Darla Fanta works as the admissions director for the Montessori School System in Sugar Land, Texas. She begins to build relationships with the school's future families from the first time they meet. Darla captures their contact information, puts it into her smartphone, and immediately sends a card from her phone with the SendOutCards app. She thanks them for spending time at the school, and says she looks forward to them becoming a part of their school family. It's become a habit that extends beyond her school job as well. Now any time Darla meets a new person, she automatically sends a "nice to meet you" card.

It's the little things that mean so much to people. When someone walks away from meeting me in whatever way we connect, I want them to know that they are a very special person. SendOutCards has helped me do that with people; to make them feel like they really mean something and made my day and they're special.

Some time ago we had a family with two little girls who were going to come to our school in two different grades, but the dad passed away before they could move to our area. They had to wait a few months before they moved over with their mom. So I went into their classrooms and I took pictures of their classmates because I knew which classes they were going to be in. I mailed each girl a card with brownies and wrote inside the cards, "We are excited to meet you." Then I put their classmates' first names on the card so the girls would know, "Oh, here are my classmates." Their mother told me the girls loved those cards and carried them around. They were excited because it helped break the tension of, "Who's going to be in my class? I don't know anyone in my class." Instead they could say, "Oh wait, I remember that face on my card." Their mother said the girls talked about their card every day because they were so excited to be coming and they got to see their classmates before they ever got there. It helped break the ice for the children when they finally did get to the school.

I know from personal experience that children love receiving items in the mail, and often they remember those impressions for the rest of their lives. I remember receiving little handwritten notes myself as a child. What you send out, you get back in return. When you send out goodness, it comes back to you in your business, no matter what your business is.

HOME INSPECTION CONSULTANT
Brian Hannigan

Brian Hannigan is a home inspector and marketing consultant from Capistrano Beach, California, with 20 years of experience in the business. It's so important for a homebuyer to find out the heartbeat and health of a home before the transaction goes through: foundation, plumbing, electrical, roof. As with many home-related services, referrals are of key importance to home inspectors.

A tremendous amount of business in my field comes from real estate agent referrals. You have to be a professional and be very good at your job, but you have to create a relationship just to get in the door at real estate offices. I network constantly, and follow up with a card and small gift as well as making connections on social media. Facebook is especially rich with life moments, opportunities for what I call social tangible touches. Look for something that's important in someone's life, whether it's the birth of a child, the death of a dog, little Johnny hitting a home run. Everybody else is going to comment on the social media post or give it a "like," something along those lines. But if you take the picture they post, drop it on a card, add a few nice words, and mail it to them, it will stand out like nothing else.

One of the inspectors I'm connected with posted a picture of his new grandchild on Facebook. So while everybody else made a little comment and liked his post, I captured the picture, put it on a card, and mailed it to him. I spoke recently at the American Society of Home Inspectors conference where there are about 2,000 people and a big exhibit hall. That inspector tracked me down to thank me personally for sending the card. How many people do you think he tracked down to say, "Hey, thanks for that like on Facebook"? He found me and personally thanked me for that card, and told me how much he appreciated it. And a deeper connection was made.

About 10 years ago, I also sent out a card to someone who paid an invoice on time. I'd just been introduced to the SendOutCards system, and had learned about the importance of appreciation, so I thought I'd give it a try. I chose a stock catalog thank you card, and wrote, "Tom, I really appreciate you paying your bill on time. You've been a great customer. Thank you very much. Look forward to seeing you soon." About a week later, I got a phone call from Tom saying, "Hey, Brian. I just got your thank you card and I wanted to thank you for it. Of all the services I have, nobody has ever thanked me for paying my bill."

I said, "Well Tom, thank you for calling to thank me for mailing you the thank you card. I appreciate it." We both had a good laugh over it, but that was my first card and the light bulb about the importance of appreciating people went off. I have become a faithful card sender because I can see how important it is to people.

Appreciating people with a tangible card is a touch many people have lost, but people crave being appreciated. If you've ever gone to your mailbox and you've seen an envelope containing a card, there's magic in that, before you even see the actual card.

CHILDREN'S ENTERTAINMENT BUSINESS
Laura Viskovich

Relationship marketing is about celebrating the people in your life. Business is always secondary to that. Laura Viskovich, who owns a children's entertainment business, Fairy La La Land, based in Sydney, Australia, is masterful at celebrating the people in her life. Her business thrives because of it. A lot of businesses, unfortunately, don't focus on customer retention or appreciation. They focus solely on getting the customer into their business. But when Laura came into contact with the relationship marketing principles at the heart of SendOutCards, she realized the focus needs to be on appreciating existing customers.

Fairy La La Land is a magical world filled with characters like fairies, pirates, princesses, and clowns. We put on children's parties and provide entertainment for children's shows around Australia, entertaining them with magic, party games, face painting, and balloon twisting. We occasionally have a mermaid pop out of the ocean at different parks around Sydney.

When a booking comes in, my virtual assistant activates a five-card touch campaign. The first one goes out to the birthday child before their booked event. I send them a card from either Mermaid La La or Ninja from La La Land. In the card we let them know we can't wait to see them at their event! Then when we do arrive, the children are so excited to see us because we've gone out of our way to touch them before we even arrive. At one party, a mom said, "I just have to thank you so much for sending that card. My daughter thinks the mermaid and the ninja are actually real, and she doesn't stop touching that card. She holds it with her. She sleeps with it. She takes it around everywhere, even to day-care. She thinks you are from a magical land of La La Land."

Then three weeks after the initial service, the mom or dad gets a "Thank you so much for booking us!" card. After that, I send out a Christmas card, and an Easter card with a "Thank you so much for knowing us." And finally, a 12-month card goes out. That's the five-card touch campaign that goes out to a new customer in my business. If someone decides not to purchase an event, we still activate a two-touch card campaign. The first says, "Thanks so much for calling us. It was lovely to speak with you." And then we also send them a Christmas card.

If you are struggling in business and you're looking at ways to grow your business, just think, "What would a human be-ing do?" Don't go from strategies of trying to get a sale. Just purely come from your heart and try to connect with peo-ple on a human level and give who you are—your authentic self—to them. Because once people like you, know you, and trust you, it organically comes into a sale and then they refer people to you. For me, SendOutCards is a way of connect-ing with my customers. Get rid of the strategies, and just become your pure, authentic self. Just be you and have fun, and the sales will come.

I love this interview with Laura. Like many of our referral partners, Laura understands people need to realize that we're in business with everybody, whether they do business with you or not. It's called the business of life. You had an interaction with another human being and whether they did business with you or not, you treat that interaction with respect. You celebrate all of the people in your life. That's the key to relationship marketing. Without people, you don't have a business.

PASTOR
Joshuwa Armstrong

Joshuwa Armstrong, assistant pastor at the Second Baptist Church of Keyport, New Jersey, represents a unique niche implementing relationship marketing to enhance the relationships of his congregation.

My dad is a pastor so I've always been in church. I enjoy church, and enjoy the word of God. My degree is in Christian Counseling and Psychology. I'm also an entrepreneur and have a delivery service, and am a referral partner in Send-OutCards. I read the book *How to Sell Anything to Anybody* by Joe Girard, and as you know, he used greeting cards to build his customer base. I decided to try this also to stay in front of my customers frequently.

We have a "first time visitor" card campaign because my mother always said, "First impressions are lasting impressions." We collect the name, address, and birthday of our first-time visitors and send out a card and box of brownies.

If they're a mother, they get a card for Mother's Day. If they're a father, they get a card for Father's Day. We have

a holiday card attached to the same campaign. And everyone on our list gets a birthday card with a box of brownies,
whether they are a member of our church of not. If they're
on our list, we're going to stay in touch with them and just
let them know we're thinking about them. I also watch Facebook, so if I don't know a member's birthday, when it pops
up on social media, I get their photo from their page and
send them a card with a box of brownies.

This year we are sending out postcards with a marriage
tip to our married couples. After they have experienced the
postcard we're going to challenge them and empower them
to do the same thing for their friends and families. Every
church's question is, "How do we connect with more people without having to spend more money?" Outreach costs
money. The common denominator in bridging the gap in today's diverse world is relationships.

Our larger mission is to teach and show people how to be nice
to each other. We're one race—the human race. Our job is to
come together in all of our diversity as one human race, celebrate each other, and send our positivity out to the world. When
we do that, the walls of religion, hatred, and racism will all start
to come down.

SALES PSYCHOLOGIST
Dr. Nancy Zare

Dr. Nancy Zare is a psychologist with a Ph.D. who also has
more than 25 years of sales experience. On my show, she explained how she helps her clients prepare for the first time they
meet with someone: how to build rapport quickly, effectively,

and authentically, as well as to find ways to get a second chance with the clients that get away. Her company is Rapport Builderz—ending with a Z, for Zare.

All of us sell, even when we don't think we're selling. When we are influencing a child to pick up their clothing or do homework, or negotiating with our spouse or a partner about where to eat, all of this is sales. So I help people get into the mind of the prospect and speak their language, so they can open the door to good negotiations.

Every prospect has a personality style that demands a different approach. Within 30 to 60 seconds, I help my clients know the answer to whether it's right brain or left brain, whether they should be singing "Kumbaya" or giving facts and figures.

I was at a trade show where a business owner was demonstrating a product. We struck up a conversation and she said, "I could use your services. Call me tomorrow morning." I called her the next day, and I got voicemail. And a couple of days later, because she hadn't followed up, I was about to call again when I decided instead to use my appreciation system and send a card and enough brownies to share with her entire staff. Approximately a week later, I got a call and she said, "You're hired." I hadn't even told her what my price was! It was a $10,000 piece of business that year.

Another time I was networking and a gentleman said, "Call me in the morning. I'm interested." This time I didn't even try to call. I went to Facebook to get a photo to put on his card, and I could only find a photo of him with his children. I was a little hesitant about mixing business with personal family stuff. But it was his only picture and I took the risk. I sent the card and brownies, and sure enough, I got hired. To this day he has that card on his bulletin board. It made me realize in this digital age we have so few tangible pictures of our children. So at Christmas, I sent him an updated picture of his kids.

As people come to mind throughout the day—past clients, current clients, friends, family members, business colleagues—I send them an impromptu personalized card. I also do this for people I meet at events. You can almost always find photos on social media, put them in a card, and a few days later surprise your new contact with a card in the mail. I don't even know that we will ever do business together. That isn't the point. The point is to build the relationship. Sometimes we can have such tunnel vision that we only pursue the people we think can help us right now. But everyone has a network, and as we build relationships, these hold the key to many other relationships.

This is what relationship marketing is all about. You focus on the relationship and marketing, and the sale takes care of itself. It's not self-promotion; it's appreciation and acknowledgement that has an enormous impact on business. I encourage you to take the risk, to not think about "what's in it for me," but simply to give from your heart and send out to give.

DENTAL PRACTICE
Dee Meacham

Dee Meacham is a dental hygienist in Cupertino, California. She received an unexpected personalized card from a friend, and when she called her friend to say thanks for the card, Dee found out how to use this system herself. There's a phrase we have around my office: "Don't ask for the referral; deserve it." Dee and her co-workers have put this phrase to work in their practice.

I started sending cards to some of my personal friends, and I couldn't even believe the response I was getting. People were calling and crying—uncles and aunts I hadn't spoken to recently, even friends I hadn't seen for a while. When you think about it, sending a card and brownies is just a little gift, but it's more than that. It's the fact that someone thought about you and took the time to personalize a card and send it to you. I loved that someone appreciated me, and I immediately saw the value for my business. I knew this was going to create a culture for our staff and our office.

Our office really understands the value of appreciating people. The type of work we do can be cyclical. Insurance changes often mean changes in our patient lists. While we were thanking patients for referrals, we weren't doing much for our new patients. We want them to have a good experience because they came to us by word of mouth. We also have a base of patients who have been coming to us for years. They've held us up, had treatments done here and there, and we didn't really invest enough into those patients. We weren't really appreciating them.

So I started sending cards to my patients. Eventually I was able to share the system with the doctor I worked with, and he got it right away. This is patient appreciation that is tangible and long-lasting.

For the kids who are having their first visit and may be afraid, we can send them a card and make it about them. We send cards celebrating our clients' milestones—when they're having a baby, celebrating a special accomplishment. That's the type of relationship we like building. I have a patient who has been coming to our office for over 20 years; he's been here longer than us, because we took over the practice from someone else 15 years ago. So we made sure to give him a card that said "Happy Anniversary." But it's not for his marriage—it's for the fact that he's been "married" to us for 20 years!

Everyone in the office is coming up with ideas for cards now, not just for our welcome cards, but also for thank you cards, for when people complete treatment, for anniversaries with our practice. When we want to remind our re-care patients, we can automatically send a card or postcard with their name already inserted. It takes out so much of the guesswork, and makes it so easy.

We don't just offer a system. We're teaching a philosophy of kindness and appreciation, which Dee personifies. Marketing has its advantages, but the warmth of someone who knows you genuinely care about them makes all the difference.

MANUFACTURER'S REP
John Endries

John Endries is a manufacturer's rep for Superior Powersports Services, a motorcycle accessories business in Tampa, Florida. He had 25 years of experience in the industry, but started over a few years ago in Florida with a brand new company and no website.

At the time, I was the guy walking in off the street. Nobody had a clue who I was and it took the better part of a year for me to really get things going. I had to get in the door, do some cold-calling, and it was a big challenge.

When I started in the industry nearly 30 years ago, I used to send out handwritten birthday cards to my clients. But when I stopped being an independent rep, I stopped sending out cards. I follow a relationship marketing referral partner and she actually helped me get started up with SendOutCards, personalizing the back of the cards and setting up my contacts in the system.

So for my new customers, I went to Facebook and took every individual dealer's logo, put it on a card, and then just wrote a basic thank you message: "Dear (name), I just want to thank you so much for your business. It is greatly appreciated." And then I added my signature at the bottom and sent out 80 personalized cards, each with a box of brownies.

Since then I've been inundated with calls and emails, so the time and money I spent doing that campaign was definitely worth the investment. I also have a VIP list of people and I send them a gratitude card every month. At Thanksgiving I sent out a card, and wrote inside, "It's not only my family and friends and loved ones I'm grateful for. I'm also grateful for my customers, because they're the ones who provide me with the opportunity to create my living. Thank you once again and may you and your family have a happy and healthy holiday season." At Christmas, I sent a funny card, and inside wrote, "Hey, as I reflect upon this year to where we are today, I realize how truly blessed I am because of people like you. I want to say thank you and wish your family a Merry Christmas and Happy New Year. Here's to an amazing 2018."

Showing appreciation has become the heart of what I do. I have to back up to tell you about the first card I sent out with the system. My parents divorced when I was 17, and we've always had a good relationship. My dad isn't very emotional, so I usually send him humorous cards for birthdays and holidays.

But as I was getting into SendOutCards, my referral partner Darla kept bringing up that the system is about the heart. So I sent my dad a card with a front that said, "The best father in the world." I downloaded some photos of my dad and his wife of 25 years when they were on vacation in the UK, and I wrote this note: "Dad and Oki, there comes a point in everyone's life when you start to really appreciate your family, especially your father, and I ask myself, Wow, when was the last time I really sent a heartfelt *I love you dad*? Oki, thank you for becoming a very special part in my dad's life and feeding me until I explode with your incredible cooking every time I come to California. I love you both."

I sent that to my dad with some brownies and he called me a couple of days after getting the card and gift. It was the most emotional I've ever heard my dad in the 54 years I've been on this earth. I've gotten so much out of this relation-ship marketing system, but that one response from my dad really meant everything to me.

We teach the world the power of relationship marketing and reaching out to people in kindness without asking for anything in return. You're simply reaching out and sharing appreciation.

FRANCHISE OWNER
Debbie Miller

Debbie Miller owns a franchise retail shop, Big Frog Custom T-Shirts, in Greensburg, Pennsylvania. When she was a guest on my *Relationship Marketing Weekly* show, she was actually a brand new system user, just 30 days in to using the service that helped her get phenomenal results.

I was fresh out of college six years ago and needed a graphic design job. This business was just opening up with the previous owner, and I got hired right away. I loved the business. We have some great customers. We often start with printing one shirt, and then people come back and buy a hundred. We have designers on-site all the time so you can design a custom t-shirt any time we are open, or you can bring in photos for us to print on the shirts. And they're ready the next day. So I worked for the store for six years, and then bought a franchise from my old boss.

With franchises, you have to stick to their recommended marketing practices and logo standards. I found I needed to do a marketing event in the winter, so I used SendOutCards to do a mailer.

When I bought the franchise, it came with a database of about 8,000 people who had purchased from the store previously. So instead of trying to find new customers, I went back to our previous customers. I went through the list and ended up with 500 names based on their buying activity and recent purchases. I created a postcard designed as a coupon to bring people back into the store. It's easiest to track response with this type of card.

The card hit mailboxes Dec. 5, and when people started receiving the cards in their mailbox, they just started coming into the store. With the holidays right around the corner it was very effective in reaching people who were looking for gifts. We actually had 50 people bring in the postcards, which generated about $5,000 in incremental sales within about a two-week period of time.

Our December was a record-breaking month for our store here, thanks to the SendOutCards relationship marketing system, along with the wonderful employees who worked very hard while I was out for most of December with my new baby. We're looking forward to more months like that, and moving forward and seeing the positive results of using our tangible cards to appreciate our customers.

ENTREPRENEUR
Jeff Ezell

Jeff Ezell is an entrepreneur based in Orange County, California, He is sales manager at a busy car dealership, and also has side gigs as a magician, an entertainer, speaker, filmmaker, film distributor, and network marketer. The first question most people ask him is, "How do you do it all?"

Running the car dealership takes enormous hours. It takes time management, but also people management. A simple "Hello. How are you?" and a smile transforms a cold person—someone you don't know—instantly to a warm person. I greet people differently.

One day at the dealership we were super busy, and the finance department was backed up. So I went in to help. I grabbed a file, and started making conversation with the buyer. He asked, "What else do you do?" I told him that as the sales manager I was at the dealership a lot, but that I also work as a magician, do network marketing, and make family-friendly faith-based movies.

He mentioned that he and some friends wanted to invest in a movie but had no idea where to start. I told him I would send him a follow-up card and a DVD of our last movie. I sent him the movie, and also a card with a box of brownies, saying, "Thank you. I appreciate your time." About a week later he called and wanted to talk more.

Long story short, we got past all of the questions and he signed on as an investor to my movie. Sending a card and a small gift is so easy, but most businesspeople don't understand that investing a few dollars is really going to propel your business. You have to send the card. You have to send some appreciation, and you have to thank your customers.

AVIATION CONSULTANT
Mark Leeper

Mark Leeper is an aviation consultant near Phoenix, Arizona. He's one of several pilots in the family: his father was a United States Air Force pilot, a fighter pilot in the Korean era and also through the 60s and 70s, and his father-in-law was a World War II ace who flew P51s and Spitfires. His son is headed to the International Guard to fly F-15s.

While I also finished my flight training, I've been a salesperson and sales coach for more than 30 years. In 2000, my wife Carolyn and I formed Seabright Company. We retain great companies in aviation and primarily work with Fortune 500 flight departments through our customers. We help our clients implement a CRM system.

I learned a great lesson from my first job in sales, in the timeshare business. My mentor demonstrated on more than one occasion the importance of focusing less on the sale and more on the prospects. What are their interests? Who is in their family? Find common ground. The key to persuading people is to make them feel good.

A few years ago I made a cold call to Aviation Business Consultants International, a specialized marketing company for the aviation industry. I presented the SendOutCards system, and they signed on. We became friends and I became a referral source for them, helping them find interested leads. So I started to receive leads from Aviation Business Consultants as well. One of these leads was an advanced flight training company down in California that dealt with Fortune 500 companies. They flew over 40 aircraft in the desert and their CEO was a tremendous businessperson. He was also a helicopter pilot, one of the most highly decorated people out of Vietnam.

I had gone down in a group to talk about what they needed to do to start their sales. They were opening a new division in their company. It didn't look like anything was going to take place in that meeting. Even so, after the meeting I sent one greeting card to their CEO. I had researched him and his unit in Vietnam, found the helicopters they flew there, and put a picture of it on the card. I simply wrote, "Thank you for your service," and signed my name.

About a week later, I received a call from him. "Are you the guy that sent me the card?" I said I was, and he said he wanted to hire me and asked me to come see him again. I flew down there again. It turned into two years full of income and I also realized another dream of mine because I got to fly fighter planes down there for 14 months—I never thought I was going to be able to do that at age 55. That one card was a tremendous income and an experience I never would have had, just for complimenting someone.

One of my customers is involved in selling huge pieces of equipment for the red, green, and yellow crowd, Caterpillar and such. They use the SendOutCards system. I had the chance to meet them at the trade show and be in their booth, and I was coaching them on how to get cards out to people. A big, tall guy with a Texas hat walked up to their booth and was very interested in a piece of equipment. He said he had to leave a day early to go back to Houston, Texas, because his granddaughter was dancing in a recital.

They shook hands and he left his business card. So I said to my customer, "Hey, try this. Let's send him a card." Of course they had their laptops hooked up and we logged into the card catalog and found a nice card with a girl dancing. I said, "Just send a card out that says, 'I hope your travels were safe and I hope your granddaughter did great at her recital.' Sign your name and put your phone number at the bottom. Don't say anything about anything else."

They sent the card. About 60 days later my customer called me and said, "You know what? The guy that we sent that card to, he just made a half-million-dollar order with the company and the reason he got back to me was because of that card." Everybody else at the trade show loaded people up with brochures and bombed them with emails and all the things that we do to ship information out. But nobody shipped anything out that made him feel something. My customer did, and there's the sale.

That is relationship marketing at its very best. In sales, it's not about you. Always make it about them. It's 100 percent of the time about creating the relationships, not about closing a sale. It's about serving, not pitching. It's really important for people to make that shift and understand it's not at all about strategy or making a sale. It's about making connections with human beings.

TREE SERVICE
Dave Potter

You read about Dave Potter of Totem Tree Service in an earlier chapter. What you may have missed is that when I had him on my *Relationship Marketing Weekly* show, he was on the job, about

50 feet above the ground in his bucket truck. He has tripled his business in the last three years, nearly all due to referrals. From his unique vantage point that is sometimes over a hundred feet in the air, he takes unique photos of his customers' homes, and sends one-of-a-kind thank you cards with gifts. He's also gained an unexpected benefit of becoming a level-four card sender.

These last couple of years of sending cards of appreciation regularly has changed me as a person. I'm a lot different than I was two years ago. Now, if the job takes a little bit longer than it would have before, I'm OK with that. Maybe before I might have felt pressure to get the job done quicker and to make that money. But now what's important is creating the relationship with the clients and taking the time to make sure the job is done correctly. My crew knows that's important to me and it's important to them now as well.

We're all excited about giving: sending cards and getting those phone calls from the customers. We've become better people from doing this consistently. Appreciating, being thankful every day for the opportunity to work on people's homes, and having an abundant mindset have all played an integral part in who we are as business owners, and we are reaping the benefits from that.

I had one customer, Louie, who had just moved to his home, and he asked me to give him an estimate on removing a little hedge. When I got there, I saw it was a beautiful little hedge. I said, "Louie, you don't want to take this hedge out. This is a beautiful hedge and it's going to provide you with amazing privacy. You've got a beautiful heritage home here. Why don't you leave it?" Then I said, "Louie, do you mind if

> I take your picture?" I took his picture and sent him a card and brownies. A few days later I got a call from Louie and he said, "Dave, I just want to thank you first of all for convincing me to leave my hedge. I love it. I absolutely love it now, and those brownies were awesome. Thank you so much." Then he asked me if I could come by and trim this maple tree. I hadn't even given him a quote on it. He just wanted to connect with me and make sure I knew he appreciated the card.

Most people are out looking for the immediate sale, but in this story, Dave illustrates beautifully the strong principles of relationship marketing. He didn't get the work initially, and in fact, he talked the customer out of it! But by following up, he gained a raving fan.

WEB DESIGN CONSULTANT
Laurie Delk

Laurie Delk works as a web design and marketing consultant in Nashville, Tennessee. She is one of the top relationship marketers in the world today. After 24 years, her business is now 100 percent referral. Laurie has a finely honed habit of sending cards, and has sent more than 80,000 greeting cards to her network in the past 13 years.

> I believe in spreading happiness and kindness no matter what. So if people do business with me, great. If they don't, that's great too. We can still be friends and I can still send them happiness through the mail and digitally through Facebook and other social media. I try to text 10 people a day and just say, "Hope you have a wonderful Wednesday!" or a terrific Thursday, or something like that. I send messages

like that on Facebook through Messenger or sometimes directly to their page. Sometimes I post a selfie saying that to everybody. If I can get their mailing address, I also send them cards and sometimes gifts through the mail. I always send birthday cards if I have their birthdate.

I have the full 5,000 friends and several thousand followers on Facebook. As a result, I don't see everything in my newsfeed, because I don't stay on social media that long during the day. About once a year, I go into my Facebook settings and download all my data—all my friends and followers. Then I copy and paste that into a notepad.

During my work day, I diligently use time blocks, and usually schedule two, 15-minute time blocks on social media. In that 15 minutes I do about five minutes of posting for myself—a cute quote or something educational, and occasionally something that's related to marketing. In the next five minutes, I read messages and get through as many as I can. And in the last five minutes, I go to my notepad and take the names of a couple of people, go to their page, and like and comment on their posts. If they posted a picture of something they're celebrating, I download those pictures and I send them a congratulations card with a pack of brownies or another small gift. Then I erase them from that notepad. That way I end up connecting with every single person on my Facebook at least once a year.

I schedule 15 minutes a day to send cards. When I meet someone, I send them a "nice to meet you" card. If I do business with them, I send them a "thank you for doing business with me" card. If it's a prospective business, then I send

them, "Thank you for your time" or "Thank you for talking
to me." I send cards at either Thanksgiving or Christmas or
sometimes right in the middle of the holidays, and then I
do another one at the beginning of the year. I sort my contacts into different groups in the contact manager within the
relationship marketing system so I can choose which card
campaigns to send to each group.

Sending out appreciation has become a habit for Laurie that
she can't turn off. She is a great example of sharing kindness
even while living through a period of personal tragedy within
five years that would stop most people in their tracks. Becoming
a masterful relationship marketer is about keeping your focus
on the things you want to attract into your life, and bringing the
human race together through kindness.

REAL ESTATE INVESTOR
Beyond Wynn

Beyond Wynn is a real estate investor from Cleveland, Ohio.
He buys homes that become rental properties, both for his own
cash flow and to sell to other investors. Over the past several
years, his deal flow has become more than 90 percent referral-based.

Normally people who are real estate agents, brokers, or
investors get properties from the Multiple Listing Service
(MLS). But in the past two years, out of a total of 30 deals, I
have bought just two properties from the MLS.

I am intentional about building relationships. And when
you focus on people, they will keep you top of mind. I get
emails, texts, and social media messages about people buy-

ing and selling properties because of those relationships. With every deal I close, I send a card and brownies or a card and Starbucks gift card to everyone who was involved, whether it's someone at the bank or the people who pull permits. I plug in my contacts and leverage the system that's already been created to help people take their lives and businesses to another level. In turn, the business just follows.

When I first started 17 years ago it was all about money. Period. It wasn't until I shifted to making it ALL about relationships, to becoming intentional about relationships, that everything changed.

At first, I thought the greeting cards were "cute," and a little touchy-feely. I wasn't that interested in people or building relationships. I just wanted to get paid fast. But when I started sending cards to people I really cared about and loved, but had never told them that because I didn't know how, the response was amazing. I remember my auntie crying about a card because I had never told her how much I love her or how much I appreciated her picking me up when I was little.

I was speaking about this at an event once and people were saying, "Get to the good part." They didn't really want to hear about relationships. They wanted to hear how I flip hundreds of houses. So I said, "Listen. By a show of hands, how many people in here can make one phone call and raise $100,000, no questions asked? Pick up the phone, call somebody." Nobody raised their hand. I said, "The reason why you can't raise your hand is because you're not focused on building relationships. If you had the relationships, you could pick up the phone and raise $100,000."

When you're interested in building relationships with people, in connecting people with other people, and in sharing information and resources with people, you're going to automatically have a shift in the way you think and in the way you see the world. We all have a gift. It's our job to identify the gift, unwrap it, and share it with the world. Together we all win.

INDEPENDENT INSURANCE AGENT
Bret Weston

Bret Weston owns an insurance agency in Kaysville, Utah. As the big carriers move more to toll-free and an online presence, as an independent insurance agent, Bret finds building relationships keeps his business on track and personal. When I interviewed Bret on my *Relationship Marketing Weekly* show, I asked him what the biggest need was to elevate the insurance industry's reputation.

There's a real need for the insurance agent in today's world. Especially as people get older and acquire more assets, they look more for the advice and the relationship of dealing with an agent. The insurance industry has traditionally changed fairly slowly, but it's moving at an extreme pace right now. The agents who don't keep up and build relationships that offer real value will be the ones who fall off.

Five years ago I started tracking my customer retention ratio, and over that time, I've averaged 95 percent retention. When I first started in the business, I didn't realize how valuable it would be to track these numbers. It comes from our referral base. It starts when our customers experience what we're about, the value we can offer them. And they want to share it with their friends or families or people they do business with.

There are some key times to reach out to a customer: when they become a customer, on anniversary dates, when a claim is made, and when our office has made an error. With the environment we're in now, meeting in person with a client is very rare. So I start off by giving them a video quote where they can see my face and hear my voice. I explain the difference in coverages we're proposing.

When they do become a client, we send out a welcome packet. We send out a letter basically explaining our involvement in the community, what we offer them, the services we provide, and how we process claims. We also send a thank you card with a brownie. I do a two-week follow-up call to make sure everything is good and make sure they don't have any questions or concerns. Most often when I make this call I don't get a thank you for saving them $250 or whatever on their policy, but I do get a thank you for the brownies, which only cost me a few bucks.

When people have any sort of claim, that can be a confusing time for them. So we send them a card reassuring them that we have their back, along with a small gift of gummy bears. We try to keep it light-hearted and follow up with a call, usually a week after the card is sent out. If we make any type of mistake, we send out a card with an apology and little goodie. Our most popular card is the anniversary card we send on the date that they became our client. We send brownies, chocolates, or caramels, with a light-hearted card that says something like, "Hey, sweetheart. We're glad we're still married to you."

These cards reinforce our relationships with our clients. Our focus is to keep our retention ratio high. It's worth every penny we spend to invest into each client relationship. As their agent, I'm invested in that client's success, their protection, and their well-being.

Bret's investment in his client has become a mindset. There's something magical about sending the card and the brownies on their anniversary date, on their start date, and when a claim is made. When he does that, it strengthens the relationship. At the end of the day, the personal relationship is what separates him from the online insurance portals.

FITNESS CLUB
Jason Alles

Jason Alles of Atlanta, Georgia, owns a fitness club and is in the process of starting up several more. He has more than doubled his guest traffic and increased referral business by 300 percent by using our relationship marketing system. Guest traffic and referral business is hugely important in this industry.

Guest traffic leading to membership is the lifeblood of any club. For years, health clubs have used direct mail for advertising and marketing. But when you're spending 30, 40, 50 cents apiece, that can get pretty expensive; most clubs don't have that kind of budget. Social media helps, but ultimately, most clubs rely on their members to bring friends to the club. In turn, clubs reward their members by giving them free dues when they bring people in. But that taps your own cash flow, and free dues for a month is not something your member can see or feel—it's not tangible.

When I saw this system, I instantly knew it would be our solution. We send our members a thank you card that has a guest pass printed on the bottom. The first month we tried this, we were seeing about 20 to 30 guests per month. But as soon as I started sending out this card, we had more than 100 guests. We then started a reward system to encourage our members to bring their friends. If a person sponsors a new member, they get a thank you card and a $10 American Express gift card. If they bring two friends, they get a $25 gift card; three friends, a $50 gift card; and four friends, a $100 gift card. It's been tremendously successful and has actually turned into a contest.

The margins in the health club business are very small. There's a lot of overhead. There's no doubt in my mind that this card system saved the club I just bought. This system is inexpensive but the value it brings is phenomenal. This system wows people.

Another challenge in the health club industry that's a little different than some others is that if you go in and have a bad experience with buying a membership or personal training or something else, all of a sudden all clubs get lumped into the same category. People say things like, "Oh, I'm never going to go to a health club again." If they get food poisoning at a certain restaurant, they may never go to that particular restaurant again. But they probably won't say they're never going out to eat again.

This industry has lost sight of how to take care of its customers. There are tens of thousands of clubs around this country that could benefit by using this relationship marketing system, and it's very simple to roll out. We are in dire need of showing our customers how much we appreciate them. I love using a system that is easy and affordable and makes our customers feel appreciated. It's really simple, and that's the key.

Our relationship marketing system is helping businesses, no doubt. But it's far bigger than that. We really believe we can bring the human race together by sharing kindness with people and treating people the way they deserve to be treated.

MORTGAGE BROKER
Linda Walters

Linda Walters of Toronto, Canada, is a mortgage broker who uses our relationship marketing system to build connections in her business. She recruits a team of agents and teaches them the entire mortgage process, from offer to closing.

As with many businesses, the mortgage industry is strongly led by referrals and repeat customers. Within a year of implementing this relationship marketing system, my referral business increased by over 71 percent in one year. I sent a lot of heartfelt cards, thanking people for already working with me over the years. I'm not techy, but this system is so well-planned and easy that my daughter can do it. And she's eight.

After a year of sending cards, I found there were four in particular that I had sent out to some real estate referral sources that ended up equaling $30,000 of my income that year. Sending gifts also makes an impression. When I send a gift to a real estate office, I send a specialty crate full of treats they can share in the office. I've had real estate agents call me and say, "Hey, Jack says you're the go-to girl for my mortgages." And they usually mention the treats I sent. It makes a great impression and a buzz in the office, especially with a personalized, customized card with photos. It's brilliant. I also send follow-up cards out to real estate agents who bring me clients, and follow-up cards and gifts out to individuals who use my company to close on their new home. At our annual convention, our president introduced my team and said, "You guys need to check out what Linda Walter's team is doing because they've increased their sales by 71 percent last year."

There are so many ways you can use this system to touch people. With a drip campaign, you can upload your database and have the system send personalized messages to your clients. I have a four-card campaign. The first is "Nice to meet you" for when I first meet a couple or a family. After we have done the transaction, I send a "Thank you for the business and the opportunity to work with you" card. The third card celebrates the one-year anniversary of their home. The fourth card is a "keep in touch" card, so it has a message like, "Thinking about you and your family and I hope all is well." I run those four cards constantly for every customer. I don't do any other marketing anymore. In an industry where the pipeline, the steady flow of business, is so important, having this relationship marketing tool makes me a better business owner. If you show appreciation and gratitude, it will come back to you. If you send it over in slices, it will come back in loaves. That has happened for me.

Our relationship marketing system will generate more business for you. But make no mistake. The bigger cause here is that we're bringing people together in kindness. And that's a great thing to be a part of. Appreciate your customers and your business will take care of itself.

About the Author

Kody Bateman is the founder of the modern-day relationship marketing movement, and Founder and Chief Visionary Officer of SendOutCards, the premier relationship marketing service in the world today. Nearly 1 million users have used his systems to send more than 160 million tangible greeting cards and 12 million gifts to over 100 countries throughout the world. Kody's newest company is Sendogo, an integration system to trigger the SendOutCards relationship marketing service to work within existing CRMs.

Kody has trained hundreds of thousands of people in his relationship marketing and personal development courses, and is the author and trainer of the bestselling seminar series, *Relationship Marketing Summit.* He has interviewed hundreds of successful businesspeople on his *Relationship Marketing Weekly* shows. He has taught over 250 live courses around the world and numerous online courses that have reached over a million people.

He has a passion for celebrating the diversity of humanity and a core mission to bring the human race together. For many years, Kody has taught that there is an art to creating bonds, trust and assurance. When you take the time to build relationships, he says, the typical aspects of marketing become simplified and genuine. Relationships create an emotional one-on-one connection and a memorable experience. And that is where the real-life riches are made, internally and externally.

Kody shares his personal development philosophy in his first book *Promptings: Your Inner Guide to Making a Difference,* where he uses stories to illustrate the significance of acting on your promptings to reach out in kindness. Promptings guide you to your genius within, he explains, helping you make the difference only you can make in the world.

Kody is a visionary leader who is living his dream and travels the country teaching others to do the same. He lives in Riverton, Utah, with his wife Jodi. They have three children and six grandchildren.